# WORKING THROUGH THE GREAT RECESSION

*One Man's Adventures Taking Jobs*
*You Didn't Know Existed*

## Andrew Edwards

ISBN-10: 1478347953
ISBN-13: 9781478347958

Library of Congress Control Number: 2012921714
CreateSpace Independent Publishing Platform
North Charleston, South Carolina

*To mom and dad (Pamela and Paul)*
*and my brother, Elijah*

# TABLE OF CONTENTS

# AUTHOR'S NOTE

All of the stories in this book are based on actual jobs I worked from 2009 until 2012. Names of the companies I worked for are either not divulged or changed completely. Names of individuals have been changed to protect their privacy. In some cases real names are used because I received permission to include them prior to publication.

# INTRODUCTION

When I left for the University of Iowa in the fall of 2001, I had no idea what I wanted to do with my life. After switching majors numerous times, I finally chose accounting at the last possible second. I was told that it was the toughest major in business school and that it would open up the most opportunities. It seemed like a good enough decision at the time, but I was too focused on playing competitive ultimate Frisbee to consider the consequences of such a demanding major more thoroughly. There were tournaments every weekend all over the country, and I was busy.

The economy was doing well when I graduated and I had no trouble procuring a job. I was hired as an entry-level accountant at a commercial real estate company in Chicago. My coworkers were great and it was a solid company, but it wasn't long before I had an *Office Space* moment and became worried that I would be sitting in that office for the rest of my life. After working there for nearly three years, I gave notice and moved to Costa Rica.

I spent the first few weeks receiving one-on-one Spanish lessons, and then moved to a small town on the Pacific coast to participate in a sea turtle population restoration program. Aside from a few minor setbacks, including being robbed of all my stuff on my second day in, it was a fulfilling journey, and I improved my Spanish skills immensely. I met people from all over the world and contracted serious wanderlust. The problem was, that during the trip, I did not have a revelation as to what to do with my life.

So, I returned to Iowa at Christmastime to figure things out. I blew through most of my savings while abroad, so it was imperative that I take whatever gigs were available to stay afloat. This book picks up at that point in my life and follows my job adventures during the Great Recession.

# LIFE AT A GLACIAL PACE

A Singaporean girl named Fatima flies into my office and calls, "Androoo! Lunch! Wah Lao!"

"Sounds good. On my way."

A month ago I didn't even know where Singapore was on a map, and now my best friend is from there. I walk outside, look up at Mt. Brown, and head over to the employee dining room to see what is being offered. I grab some cereal, fruit, and a burger, eat outside with a group of people from the other side of the world, and reflect on how this came to be.

---

After returning from Costa Rica last December, I had to start thinking about what to do. Should I move back to Chicago? Stay in Des Moines? Check out the West Coast? As an outdoor enthusiast, I was drawn to websites offering jobs at national parks and similar places around the country. I was denied one job as a glacier tour guide in a remote part of Alaska. I turned down another job taking pool tickets at a lodge on the Olympic Peninsula. Then, in early January, I heard back from Glacier National Park about a location accountant position. Did I want it? Definitely.

---

A day after attending a friend's wedding in Iowa City in early May, I am ready to go and realize I won't see this state again for nearly five months; I will be in a remote part of the country with little access to the rest of the world. This intimidates me, but there is no backing out now. It takes me three days to travel the 1,500 miles to the park. I check out the Battle of the Little Bighorn memorial, drive through Badlands National Park, and go to the source of the Missouri River. My assignment is at Lake McDonald Lodge, inside the park about ten miles from the western entrance. When I arrive, the ground is still snow-covered and I am one of the first people there. I have to be trained before the lodge opens.

After bouncing around dormitories, I become roommates with a guy named Dan, who arrived around the same time. He is the assistant front desk manager, originally from Detroit, but recently living in Portland. We immediately attempt some hikes despite the fact that there are still several feet of snowpack around the lodge. One trail disappears when a flooded river gets in the way. We spend a couple of hours dangerously fording it in an attempt to pick up the trail, but to no avail. We decide to cut our losses and return to the lodge, vowing to try again later in the summer.

During the first week, two managers come to the office to train me. My office is in a hallway behind the hotel lobby. The highlight is a huge photograph above my desk of a grizzly bear with its cubs. The first manager, the controller, works on the east side of the park. He is in charge of cash handling and revenue, among other things. He shows me how to open the gigantic antique safe in my office where the money and various keys are stored. I conjure up an image of a bandit holding a gun to my head, demanding that I open the safe, but I keep forgetting the combination. I guess that's why a security guy will make a daily appearance to pick up cash. Manning the safe will be half of my job. I will provide change to different departments—gift shop, camp store, bar, two restaurants, transportation desk, and front desk—when they need it. I will not see the controller again for the rest of the summer.

My other manager is a woman who works in a nearby town and is in charge of payroll for all of the lodges throughout the park. She shows me how to operate the system to input payroll data for the 175 people employed here for the summer. After a couple of hours, I am confident I know how to do it. In fact, someone in elementary school could be proficient at this job. All I do is put numbers into boxes and press enter. I pretend I'm playing Number Munchers to spice things up.

There are also two location managers. The boss is a man in his forties named Todd who hails from Mississippi. He began work as a bellman in the park twenty years earlier and has worked his way up to head honcho. He is in charge of everything, knows the ins and outs of the place, and lives in an old cabin a hundred feet from the lodge. Donna, a woman in her sixties who is also from the south, is the assistant location manager. They work next door to me inside the lodge and I keep them updated on how the payroll hours are doing against the budget.

---

Gradually, employees start to trickle in. Unbeknownst to me, Glacier regularly recruits international workers, which makes things interesting. Each night, the different departments leave their time sheets on my door for me to complete the following day. In my early days on the job, it is chaos because nothing is alphabetized, and I can't read anybody's names because they aren't in the system. Chan Shu-Yu? Yang Yu-Hui? Fortunately, all of the Chinese and Taiwanese also have Western names. For example, Liao Chen-Hui is "Celia," and Tien I-Chia is "Crystal." Some Slovakian and Czech last names are about twenty letters long. There are people from Kazakhstan, China, Japan, Singapore, Malaysia, Vietnam, Taiwan, the Czech Republic, Slovakia, France, Austria, Germany, Jamaica, Switzerland, and Turkey, among others. The internationals make up about forty percent of the work force; the rest are Americans. Most of the employees are students or are in their twenties, but there are a few exceptions. There is a waiter who has worked here longer than Todd and returns every summer. A few other servers have been here for several summers because of the easy schedules and good tips.

Many of the employees are active and outdoorsy. The manager of the gift shop is a hippy in her fifties or sixties. Every year, she organizes a hike to Avalanche Lake to kick off the summer. This is one of the most scenic hikes in the park and is also one of the easiest. This time, it ends up

5

being her, all of the Singaporeans, and me. This is where I meet Fatima and she immediately begins to educate me on Singapore, a place that seems light-years ahead of the United States in technology, education, infrastructure, and just about everything else. The one thing that Singapore lacks is wilderness, since it is a huge city on an island. This proves evident when, halfway up the trail, a deer runs by and everyone goes nuts.

"We have only seen these special creatures in zoos!" they cry in excitement.

I explain to them that deer are a nuisance, and that there are millions of them in this country. In fact, I have been in two cars that have hit deer, each time totaling the vehicle. I tell them that they will see plenty of deer and that it is no big deal.

Fatima and I arrive way ahead of the rest of the crew because we were flying up the trail (her penchant for walking fast and taking risks meshes well with my style, and we end up hiking together numerous times over the first two months of the summer). The view at the top is amazing. There is snow everywhere and several waterfalls crash into the lake. We can see mountain goats maneuvering about the cliff. I will end up doing this hike half a dozen times this summer and never tire of it.

———————

The job becomes frustrating because the payroll system has to be done online. Since we are nowhere near civilization we must use a satellite connection, which moves at a snail's pace. I click someone's name and wait. And wait. There we go. I put in a number and click enter. Then I wait some more. I click submit and move to the next person. For 175 employees, a job that should take an hour drags into three or four. Between mouse clicks my eyes wander over to the grizzly bears on the wall, and I wonder if I will see any this summer. Even with the slow connection, I finish early in the day. I am scheduled for eight hours and don't know what else I am supposed to do. I guess that I am here for when things go wrong or for when people need to make change, but both of these scenarios are rare. So, I stroll around the lodge, looking up at the impressive collection of mounted animal heads in the main lounge. There are bears, mountain goats, bighorn sheep, and others. I walk behind the lodge and check out Lake McDonald. The back of the lodge was originally the front. There wasn't a road into the park until a few decades ago, so the only way to get here was by boat (one of many interesting facts you can learn by taking a boat tour run by the Glacier Boat Company).

It's not always routine. One day, Todd walks into my office.

"All right, a couple of payroll changes. Mary and Bill are gone. Got caught by the NPS smoking weed. Oh, and Mike is also out of here. He was wasted and broke into the kitchen last night trying to get some food." I make the appropriate changes.

Besides the international students, there is another contingent of employees working here: the hard partiers who like to hang out in the rec room into the wee hours of the morning. There are about twenty of these people and most of them work in the restaurant. When they get off late at night, they go to the rec room to drink beer, play pool, and listen to music until two or three in the morning. They also go to West Glacier, the pseudo-town on the edge of the park, to visit Frida's, a bar that brings in raft guides, local seasonal workers, and our employees.

I make a fair number of appearances at the rec hall myself, mainly to play ping-pong or to watch tennis on TV. There are a lot of good ping-pong players here. The Jamaican dude puts a nasty spin on his shots, and the Taiwanese contingent can hold their own by using the traditional Chinese grip. The Czech guys don't mess around either. However, it is the Texan who drives one of the historic red buses that has my number. I have beaten everyone in the park except for him. One night, I have my best chance and am up 20–16, game point to me. I crumble under the pressure and he beats me, 23–21.

I go to the rec room every few days to hit the ball around with Fatima. She is a natural at ping-pong, but we never actually play a real game, preferring instead to stick to volleying without keeping score. Fatima becomes my partner in crime for many reasons. She is the only person I have met who can walk as fast as me, the only girl that I have never had to wait on, and most importantly, she is always down for an adventure, even when it has all the signs of a bad idea. We recently infuriated our friends, Izzah and Yvonne, by inviting them to the Howe Lake trail, arguably the worst hike in the park. It was overgrown, full of biting mosquitoes, and had no appealing features. The girls turned back right at the beginning, and waited three hours for Fatima and me to finish, worrying themselves sick in the process.

———

More problems arise in the accounting office.

"Hi Andrew. My check. No correct. No my position." There is an international employee in my office telling me his check is wrong. It turns out that this is not unusual, but because different jobs have different pay, it does matter. Everyone is assigned a position in the system when they are hired, but most of the time they end up moving to a different job altogether, depending on needs. Unfortunately for me, the managers never find it necessary to inform me of these changes, so I have to retroactively change their pay for all of the weeks they have been filed under the wrong job. At least when this happens, it breaks the monotony of data entry, giving me an opportunity to meet some of the other employees.

One guy was hired as a second cook but has effectively been working as a first cook since the beginning of the summer. With the pay differential he is owed about $1,500, so I tell him this when he brings it up, and then report the finding to Todd. It becomes a big deal, and in the end, the higher-ups say that the guy won't get paid the difference and don't really give me a reason. I awkwardly inform the cook a few days later that he will not be compensated for the $1,500 after all.

———

My roommate, Dan, is promoted less than two weeks into the season. The previous manager had a gambling addiction and would disappear into town, then come back to work a day late looking like he hadn't slept in days. The head of housekeeping was also promptly replaced; she wanted to take a leave of absence, but when this was not allowed, she quit. The pizza place also had to be re-staffed. The original manager was gung ho about the season. In a meeting during the first week, he said everything would be ready to go for opening day. A couple days later, he disappeared in the middle of the night and no one heard from him again. As a result, the new manager came into my office and asked if I knew someone who could translate Mandarin for him. I told him I knew just the person.

Fatima did not want to do this, but she was too nice to say no. The manager wanted to have a meeting, and since his entire work squadron hailed from China and Taiwan, he wanted everything to be clear. Fatima told me that it was super-awkward because all of the workers understood English.

———————

Halfway through the summer, I somehow become a travel agent. This is the first year the park has ever made Wi-Fi available, but it doesn't work. The only person within a twenty-mile radius who has somewhat reliable Internet access is me. This information gets out fast, much to the chagrin of Todd. He has already yelled at me several times for having Fatima and Izzah hanging out in my office, and now I have a steady parade of internationals looking up travel ideas on my computer. It begins with a couple of Chinese women that come in to see if I can help them get to Las Vegas. I use my travel savvy to get them a flight on a discount airline. A few days later, the housekeeping manager asks me where Summer (her Western name) and Yan are. I tell the manager that they are in Vegas.

"Yeah, I know, but they were supposed to be back yesterday and are scheduled to work today." *Uh oh.* Neither of them have cell phones that work in this country, nor is there a way to get hold of them. Disaster is averted when they make it back the next day. They missed their plane, which only flies once a day. The managers are not happy, but apparently the girls had a good time.

I start booking trips for all sorts of people. Many of the internationals don't have working credit cards, so I pay for their tickets and they reimburse me in cash. The Jamaican wants an iPod and other electronics that are much cheaper in the United States, so I buy them for him and he pays me back. I feel like Red in *Shawshank Redemption*—I am the guy who knows how to get things. One of my key luxuries is a car, because the nearest town, Kalispell, is forty-five minutes away. This is where we stock up on power bars, goldfish crackers, gummy worms, and booze. It is also where we can go to visit Internet cafes, watch movies, and enjoy some "fine dining." Every couple of weeks I take a crew into town, as I have added chauffer to my assorted duties. The Singaporeans love Walmart because it is cheap, and they stock up on everything.

When I discover that some of the girls will leave soon, I orchestrate a trip with Dan, Fatima, Izzah, and Yvonne. There is another national park connected to Glacier, but on the Canadian side, called Waterton National Park. I ambitiously suggest we go there for two nights, then go up to Calgary for the famed Stampede[1], then drive through Banff and Kootenay National Parks, then hit up Radium Hot Springs on the way back, all before returning for work four days later. Fatima, Izzah, and Yvonne need to obtain special visas to cross over into Canada and they get them just in time.

We complete a unique hike in which we take a ferry across Waterton Lake to get to the trailhead. The trail is called Crypt Lake, and it winds through the forest until it reaches a valley, where we have to climb a ladder and go through a short tunnel. Eventually, we get to the lake, which straddles the United States–Canada border. We see our first marmots, which are goofy looking rodents the size of a beaver.

The park is great, but I am underwhelmed by the Stampede in Calgary. It is the largest rodeo in the world, but it is not much different from the Iowa State Fair[2]. The girls love it because the outlandishly unhealthy food, high dive shows, giant horses, and exhibits are completely foreign to them. We drive through Banff and do another couple of day hikes, ending up at one of the more famous lodges, the centerpiece of the park. Yvonne inquires about employment there for next summer.

---

1 The Calgary Stampede is an annual rodeo festival that draws over a million visitors a year.
2 See "Bad State of A Fair"

We drive through Kootenay and do one last hike. In the afternoon, we go to Radium Hot Springs, which is not exactly what I expected. I want natural trails leading to pockets of super-hot water holes, but instead it is family central. There is one huge hot spring pool and one big cold-water pool. Still, a hot spring is a hot spring, so it suffices. We leave in the evening and have to get back to Glacier in order to work the next day. Towards the border, I start hallucinating from exhaustion and swear that I see hundreds of deer everywhere. We are in the middle of nowhere, taking a back road down to the border. I do everything I can to stay awake, and we return to the lodge at three in the morning.

––––––––––––––

The time has come for Fatima and Izzah to leave so that they can return to school in Singapore. I take them to Apgar Village, the small town site inside the park, so we can have one last huckleberry cobbler. I have gone on over a dozen hikes with them in a short period of time, especially with Fatima, who will have scars on her legs from our shenanigans for a long time. We did a lot of suspect things, like hiking the High Line trail with a thunderstorm overhead, trying to climb to the peak of one of the local mountains, and hiking at night on more than one occasion. Our tradition is to get pie and huckleberry cobbler at various restaurants in and outside the park after each hike. Even though they aren't leaving until tomorrow, I have to get to Missoula for an ultimate tournament, so this is my last chance to see them. Since Fatima has become my best friend, this is a hard goodbye. I say I'll see them again at some point, and then hit the road.

––––––––––––––

I got in touch with the ultimate community out here before I made the trip. I end up playing with a Missoula team at tournaments in Bozeman, Missoula, and Lake Coeur d' Alene. Missoula is not very big, but it has a huge ultimate community. We field three teams in Bozeman, and one of them wins the tourney. The top mixed team wins sectionals in Missoula, and we also have a team win the Idaho tournament.

Inside the park, I try to throw the disc around as much as possible with anybody who is willing. One guy I throw with works in housekeeping and is in the process of getting his master's degree in religious studies at Princeton. Another guy who throws with us will be an architect. These situations are par for the course with this place. Fatima is finishing up her law degree at one of the top law schools in the world and speaks four languages fluently. Another girl in housekeeping is getting her MBA in the United States. Yvonne has her master's in sports economics. My friends from Germany speak better English than I do because they are going to be English teachers. One of them, Ane, shows me her thesis and asks me for help. I tell her it looks perfect, because I have no idea how it can be improved. My two friends from Taiwan who are in housekeeping will both be accountants in Taipei for Deloitte and Touche, a Big Four accounting firm. Valerie, another good friend from Singapore, will be a brand manager for a major marketing firm. Their accomplishments and ambitions go on and on. It is interesting to think about how many of the Americans who have better jobs at the lodge will end up being unemployed in three months, while the internationals in housekeeping will have great jobs when they return home.

————————

In the middle of the summer there is the annual Chili Cook-Off at East Glacier on the other side of the park, which is where the main lodge and offices are. Dan takes part in the pie-eating contest, and we play volleyball for a couple of hours. Later in the night, I am with Dan and four Taiwanese girls, all crammed into the backseat of my car. There is supposedly an after-party—some sort of bonfire thing. I drive down a labyrinth of roads until we find a clearing, but it is not the correct place. The roads are terrible, and I feel like my car is going to be destroyed by one of the gigantic potholes dotting the road. I decide to call it a night and make the treacherous trip back to the west side on Highway 2. No less than three Lake McDonald people have nailed a deer this summer, but we make it back safely and go to bed.

The next day, there is a buzz throughout the lodge about the previous night. Apparently, there was a huge brawl at the after-party. Talk is, someone has lost a finger and a dozen people are in the hospital. Levi, one of the maintenance guys, is either arrested or in the hospital. No one has seen him. The next day, people still haven't seen him. Finally, he shows up, and we ask what happened. He claims to have no idea what we are talking about. Apparently, he left the bonfire because not much was going on, and visited a friend's place outside the park for a couple of days. Although the rumors spiraled way out of control, the brawl really did happen. It involved a couple of Glacier people, but east side people, not west side workers.

Adjacent to the east side of the park is a huge Native American reservation for the Blackfeet Tribe. It is a very poor area, and there are often skirmishes between local Indians and Glacier workers. Apparently, one of the girls from the reservation hit a guy from East Glacier and all hell broke loose, but the rumors of a dozen people in the hospital and a guy losing a finger turn out to be fictitious. A couple people have bruises, but that is it. This is something that will never happen on our side of the park; ping-pong, marijuana, drinking, volleyball, reading by the lake, hiking, and peaceful bonfires are what we are all about.

---

As the summer progresses, Dan and I decide to up the ante on our hikes. We opt to do what most sane people don't even consider—the Nyack Loop. In order to complete this hike, we have to drive to some random spot off of Highway 2 outside the park, leave our car, cross the river (the same river used for the whitewater rafting trips), and traipse over fifty miles through untouched wilderness. This is the only part of the park that has a special designation that allows people to camp anywhere, as opposed to specific campgrounds, because so few people attempt it in a given year.

When I go to the backcountry permit office and explain my itinerary, the bearded park ranger looks at me and says, "Are you out of your mind?"

"Maybe, but it's something we have to do." He doesn't have to let us go, but he does. Early last summer, a guy walked in and turned in an incredibly ambitious itinerary for a ten-day hike. It was approved and that was the last time anybody saw him. He never made it to the first campsite. There are all sorts of theories, but he probably fell through a crevice while walking over snowpack and disappeared forever. This won't happen to us because it is the hottest part of the summer. If we have any problems they will be bear or heat related.

We leave on a Friday afternoon right after work and the goal is to come back Sunday afternoon—fifty miles in less than 48 hours. It takes us an hour to find the trail entrance and we are already off to a bad start. It is evident that no one has hiked this trail all summer, even though it is late July. We cross the same river about ten times, and each time, I take off my shoes so they don't get wet. Eventually, I get sick of doing this, so I decide to walk through, which proves to be a rookie mistake. Wet feet cause blisters, and blisters can ruin hiking trips quickly. This part of the trip is brutal. The trail is completely overgrown, and there is nothing to see but trees all around us. We manage to make it to the campground safely and immediately crash in our tent.

The second day is more scenic as the trail opens up a bit. Early in the morning, we are on the edge of a valley that goes down to the river we just camped next to. Dan is in front of me and when we turn a corner, a huge black bear is trotting down the trail towards us.

"Black bear in front of us," I say.

"What?"

"Look up." Dan stops and starts walking backwards.

"Okaaaay . . . what do we do?"

"Grab your bear spray." He grabs it and stands ready. The bear looks up and clearly hasn't seen humans in a long time and darts off into the woods.

*Okay, black bears. Not a big deal.*

The second campground is the highlight of the trail. There are two lakes in an open valley and a tall waterfall feeds one of them. We get there early enough so we can explore and leave our stuff at the campsite. We have to wade across an ice-cold channel and climb over a hill separating the lakes. Later, I am standing near the edge of the lake when a three-inch long leech crawls out of the water and onto my foot.

"All right, Dan, maybe we should head back."

When we return to the campsite, I look at the clothes I had put out to dry. My belt has been chewed in half and my boxers are completely destroyed. It looks like something has tried to do the same to my pants as well. I still don't know what did it, but I am guessing a deer, squirrel, or marmot. They like salty things and can smell sweaty clothes from miles away. We talk about the bear incident, and Dan decides to practice with the bear spray.

"Is that a good . . . ?" I start to say. Seconds later, my eyes, nose, and mouth are burning. The wind has pushed the pepper into my face.

"Fuck!" I start coughing and can't breathe. Dan tells me to settle down—it can't be that bad. Maybe not, but I cough the rest of the night. I fall asleep thinking that, despite a few mishaps, the Nyack Loop hasn't been too bad.

Then, we hit day three. Twenty miles to go, and my feet are covered with blisters and my back is killing me from carrying my pack. The sun beats down on us and there is no shade to be found. We have to painstakingly navigate through areas where avalanches have knocked down hundreds of trees. Our rations are low, but we find some berries to eat and they give us enough energy to keep pushing. A few miles later we see people for the first time since Friday afternoon and they are amazed to see us. It is a large team of AmeriCorps volunteers clearing the trail, a task long overdue. The path opens up and is much easier to walk on, but it barely helps because we are so tired. We get to a fork in the trail, just a few miles from civilization.

Now comes decision time. We can hike the five miles back to our car through dense foliage or cross the river at a more dangerous point and hitchhike back. In our current condition, it's an easy call and we head for the river. It is moving fast, so I choose to go at a narrow point. I almost fall over a few times, but gradually make it across. I look back to see Dan looking at me.

"I'm going to try at a different point," he says, moving along the riverbank. I sit down and wait for him. After a few minutes, I walk down and see him sitting on a huge boulder in middle of the river with water rushing by on both sides. The water had suddenly gotten deep, so he climbed onto the rock to think about his next move.

Dan plans to jump off of the rock without his bag and swim to me. The current pushes him downstream about fifty feet before he gets out. He takes rope from me and goes back upriver and jumps in again. This time, the current pushes him into the rock. He ties the rope around his waist and the bag. He then repeats the same maneuver to get across. I film the entire debacle for safekeeping and for future blackmail material.

Once Dan recovers from his ill-conceived river crossing, we scramble up a hill to get to the highway. It's the home stretch. We are out of food and dehydrated, so we begin to solicit any vehicle that we see. Not many cars are going by and we have no luck getting one to pull over. After walking for several minutes, I look back, and Dan has vanished. I decide to stop, and after two hours, a family of Mexicans pulls over in a truck.

My Spanish comes in handy. "Gracias. Mi carro está cinco millas por allá." He seems to understand and begins to drive. A couple miles up the road, there is a desperate looking guy holding up his thumb—Dan.

*How did he get ahead of me?*

He jumps in, and we don't say anything. We are let off at our car, and we drive back to Glacier. I feel like I have just gotten back from a war zone. We manage to arrive in time for dinner, and then I crash. I am not able to hike for nearly two weeks because my feet hurt so badly from the blisters. Despite my suffering, the experience supplies me with ample bragging rights about hikes.

People will be eating in the dining room and someone will say, "We just did Avalanche Lake. Have you done any hikes lately?"

There will be a pause as I slowly make eye contact.

Then, I'll reply, "Actually, yeah. The Nyack Loop. EVER. FUCKIN'. HEARD OF IT! Not a big deal. Bears everywhere, avalanches, leeches, raging rivers, fifty miles in forty-eight hours, hitchhiking, dehydration, blisters, and bushwhacking the ENTIRE time. Yeah, we've done some hiking lately."

---

A couple weeks later, after my blisters have healed, I go on a hike with my Taiwanese friends, which is something they haven't done much of this summer. The only hikes they do are ones to the local shopping malls. I drive around to pick them up, and am appalled at what I see. They are decked out in colorful canvas sneakers, skinny jeans, and oversized sunglasses. Their Gucci cross-body bags contain small plastic bottled waters.

"Guys, you know we're going on a hike, right?" The hike involves quite a bit of climbing, but they do manage, albeit at a much slower pace. This is partly because they are walking slowly, but mostly because they are taking millions of pictures. They record every possible combination of angles and people: Karen with Mika; Karen, Mika, and Irene; Rahman and Su only; Andrew with everyone; Andrew with Irene; Irene and Mika only.

The photo shoot continues until I say, "Guys, the sun doesn't stay up until eleven anymore. We have to get moving."

---

My accounting job is just a side project at this point. It takes me so little time to do my actual work that all I do is plan hikes, rafting trips, bonfires, volleyball games, ping-pong tournaments, and trips for the internationals. Then one day, something unusual happens. I get a call in my office from a woman who is hysterical. It is the aunt of a young boy who went kayaking earlier in the day and hasn't returned. There are private historic cabins on the other side of Lake McDonald, and apparently, the kid and his parents had been visiting there with the aunt. The parents had left a couple days earlier, but the aunt stuck around with the kid for a few extra days.

It has been a very windy day, so the water is extremely choppy. I tell her to calm down and that we will figure it out. I go from typing numbers in boxes to being a 911 dispatcher. I take down the boy's description and name and have her email me a picture of him. I make a poster, and we print copies and post them around the lodge. The aunt has called the National Park Service (NPS) to begin a search. I tell her I will call her with updates. I go outside and find out that the tour boat people have been following the situation. There is now a helicopter circling the lake. Then, an NPS boat comes back with a kayak attached to it—an empty kayak.

*Yeesh.*

I talk to Todd and he says to call the aunt to give her the information for the NPS and to tell her it is out of our hands. I call her back but make no mention of the empty kayak. I don't want to give her a heart attack. It is the right decision, because the situation is quickly remedied. The boy is found at the edge of the lake waving for help. Apparently, he was thrown out of the kayak because the waves had gotten too big, and he swam to shore.

———————

Every year, one or two people die in the park for a variety of reasons. This year, a motorcyclist died after flying off a cliff on a curve. The week I arrived at McDonald Lodge, a man was chased down by a bear, but survived. He drove himself to a local hospital and was released with minor injuries. Most of the other injuries are fairly minor, like twisted ankles or hypothermia. My friend Ane stepped over a ledge and twisted her ankle, which put her out of hiking action for a few weeks. Another girl nearly broke her foot stepping in a ground squirrel hole.

The craziest encounter of my summer occurs with the least likely people in the least likely location. My parents decide to visit in early August and stay a few nights. They plan to hang out on their own for a few days, and I will join them when I can. After doing a hike during their first day in the park, we have enough time to do the loop trail around Swiftcurrent Lake. This is a small lake right next to Many Glacier Lodge, a huge building in the northeast part of the park. This is a trail that anybody can hike. It is late in the afternoon so it is the best option while we still have daylight.

We begin at the lodge and start to walk around the trail. Not another soul is in sight, which is nice for now. After about forty minutes, we are nearly done. I cross a bridge over a creek that feeds into the lake. I walk a hundred feet and turn the corner. My mom points out two animals close to the trail.

"Look, a couple of sheep or something."

"Not quite. Those are grizzly bears. Let's back up behind this corner. Let me think." The bears see us and get up on their hind legs. There are two of them and they are big. In the first week, all of the employees have mandatory wilderness training, with about ninety percent of the course devoted to bears. It was so long ago that I can't remember what to do. When hiking, you are supposed to be noisy so you don't sneak up on bears, but sneak up on them is just what we did. So I figure that we should make noise as if we were hiking around the corner for the first time. We start yelling and clapping from around the corner, but the bears don't do anything except continue to look in our direction. This isn't working. Fuck it. Let's play it safe.

"Let's turn around and bomb back to the lodge. We still have a little daylight." We walk over the bridge. I turn to the left and there is another huge grizzly walking down the path towards me. My heart starts to beat hard and fast. To my left are woods that lead about twenty feet straight down to the lake, but the river cuts off that route. To my right is a forty-five degree incline into no man's land. The only option is to turn around and go back across the bridge.

"What are you doing?" my dad asks.

"Huge grizzly coming our way. We have to turn around."

"Are you kidding me?" he asks, with panic in his eyes.

"No. And there's not much time." I tell them we have to yell and scream and clap as loud as possible to see if these bears will move. I am pretty sure the bear I just saw is the mother, and if there is one thing I remember from bear training, it is that mother bears don't like it when other animals are near their cubs. My dad starts screaming for help, and the situation has suddenly become very real.

Once again, the bears just stand up on their hind legs and look our way. I don't know what to do now. We are going to be a small blip in the news tomorrow. There is the lake on our right and thick brush to our left, with a hill back behind us. I know that bears are much faster than humans, especially my parents.

"All right, we will just have to walk by these bears. Keep your head down, don't look at them, and mutter to yourself softly. Whatever it takes to indicate that you aren't a threat." There is no more time for thinking, so I begin to walk. The standing bear is over six feet tall on its hind legs, and I can feel his eyes on me as I walk right by him. The bears are just a few feet from me and I am interrupting their feast. My heart is going to burst out of my body.

"Just walking here, bears. Don't mind me," I mutter. I am by them. I turn around and see nothing but fear in both of my parents' eyes. I think the mother bear will turn the corner any second now, so I wave at them to hurry the fuck up. They go in single file, and as if in slow motion, walk right by the bears. We make it and quickly turn another corner, and no one says a word. We are all shaking with adrenaline. Less than two minutes later we come to a clearing where there are about twenty people in a parking lot listening to loud music and grilling. We were literally three hundred feet from them, but because of the music, they couldn't hear any of our shouts. There is a trail that continues next to the lake, but we decide to take the road. The sun is almost completely gone, another factor that has made the last few minutes a harrowing experience.

My parents are not happy with me. This is not the kind of hike they wanted to do on their vacation. But we regroup in Many Glacier Lodge and grab beers in the lounge. I see a tour bus driver I know and we tell him the story, and he can't believe it.

"There are never really many bears right on the Swiftcurrent Trail— too many people. And if there are, they usually just run away."

Yeah, these bears weren't running anywhere. We report the incident to the local information desk so that they can let people know there are bears on the popular trail.

After reflecting on this bear experience, I realize that I have a penchant for getting into situations like this. Like the time when I persuaded my dad to go to Bull Island off of the South Carolina coast, where there are over 1,000 alligators on a six-mile long island. On the path we went on, with water on all sides, we came upon a fifteen-foot alligator that wasn't moving. It was right in middle of the footpath. I got within ten feet of it, and it just stared at me. I decided that we could backtrack and go down a different route. On the next path, there were more alligators—dozens of even bigger ones. But these slid off into the swamp on either side, and we were like Moses parting the Red Sea. When we finally got to the ocean, all of the other people from the ferry were already there. We asked them how they got by the alligator that wasn't moving, but they didn't know what we were talking about. They said there weren't any alligators on the main path.

Then there was the time when my friend Joe and I got lost in the Mexican desert and ran out of water, miles from the nearest town. And the time I had to beg for food in Costa Rica after hiking twenty-five miles through thick jungle inside a remote national park. Then there was the time in Panama a few months ago, when I was lost for several hours on a trail and recorded a final message on my camera in case I didn't survive.

And then there was my college graduation trip, when I was stuck on a remote island in Alaska for an entire day. I got mixed up with an insane guide who was trying to teach self-sufficiency in the wild. He turned out to be a con artist, so I fled town to get away from him. And apparently, Joe and I didn't learn our lesson with deserts because we ended up getting lost again in Joshua Tree National Park the year after our Mexican debacle and hiked over twenty miles on sand. The list goes on and on and on.

I realize that I am the nucleus, the epicenter if you will, of bad decisions. Fording raging rivers unnecessarily, hiking at night numerous times, crossing dangerous Mexican border towns famous for daily beheadings, hitchhiking with strangers in foreign countries, sea kayaking in near hurricane conditions, tubing down flooded rivers on inflatable rafts, and trespassing on private land in Costa Rica and getting hunted down and almost shot. It is this bear experience that finally made me recognize the pattern. I vow to carry bear spray with me for the rest of the summer.

One last incident occurs on the job front. The bar manager, John, has been trouble all summer. It turns out that he has never worked as a bartender. He lied on his application to get the job. Early on, his friends from Texas visited and took over the rec room, drinking and carrying on all night. Now, a couple months later, they have come back. I show up in the morning and am doing payroll when one of the bigwigs from East Glacier comes by.

"Can you open the drop-box and see if the bar made their drop last night?" I open it up and there is nothing there. "That's what I thought."

She tells me that last night while John was working, he and his buddies drank for free all night. He was ignoring customers and reportedly threw a blender at the wall because he couldn't get it to work. A couple of patrons complained about him to the front desk.

She tells Todd, and he calls the NPS to help with the situation. If John had left town he probably could have gotten away, but instead, he is still passed out from the night before. He lives next door to me, where I heard knocking earlier in the morning, but apparently he didn't answer. Now, the NPS guys and Todd try again, and sure enough, they find over $1,000 in John's room. He saw the writing on the wall and was going to make a break for it. Todd tells John that he should be arrested, but instead gives him and his friends an hour to get off the property. John gets the message and takes off only to be arrested a couple days later in the eastern part of the park, where he and his friends are caught smoking weed in a hotel room.

At my count, over half of the original managers have been fired throughout the summer. At each weekly meeting, Todd insists that whatever it takes, we will "get it right" with regards to the management team. People are still being shuffled around and there are only a couple of weeks left in the season.

---

Many of the internationals are leaving soon, so I try to give them a memorable last hurrah. A huge cowboy bar outside the park has karaoke on the weekends, and I convince the Taiwanese crew to come along to experience American-style karaoke before the summer ends. The place hosts rodeos throughout the year and is decorated with glass cases containing real grizzly bears that were killed in Alaska. People generally sing country western songs, but in a weird twist, the DJ plays club music between turns. Patrons jump up and dance for a couple minutes and then sit back down when the bass is overtaken by acoustic guitar. I sing a Weezer song with Dan, but the Taiwanese refuse to sing, since they are used to singing in private rooms with friends—not in front of a hundred strangers. After Mika dances with a real American cowboy and we sing another couple songs, we head back to the park.

Dan and I decide to supplement the karaoke trip with a huge bash for all the people leaving the country. We organized a bonfire earlier in the summer that was pretty fun, but this time, it's got to be perfect. We run it by Todd, and he's game.

"Anything to keep employee morale up at the end of the summer."

I tell him we would appreciate some company cash to bankroll the party.

"Sure, how much? Fifty bucks?"

"We were thinking $200."

"Whoa, whoa, whoa. Easy guys." He gives us $100, offers up food and two grills from the kitchen, and authorizes maintenance to provide us with a bunch of firewood. The rest is up to Dan and me. We go to town and buy more food and drinks. We decide to chip in our own money to load up on beer because running out would be embarrassing. The end-of-the-summer-party has to be memorable.

I make posters and put them up everywhere. I talk to the Eastern Europeans, the Asians, the hippies, the alcoholics, the religious zealots, the nerds, the older people, the boat people, and even the horse stable workers.

"You have to come," I keep saying. I get Tim, the assistant manager for the camp store, to DJ for the party. He has all sorts of professional DJ equipment and has performed at numerous bars throughout the summer.

The day arrives, and we begin with a volleyball game next to the fire pit. After we finish, a friend named Paul, from Minnesota, starts the bonfire. Tim sets up his equipment and starts the music and people gradually make their way over. Two volunteers run the grills. We have burgers, veggie burgers, brats, all sorts of chips and cookies, and a bunch of beer. It is about 10:00 p.m., and almost everyone has made an appearance, except for my Taiwanese crew. When they finally come, it is obvious that they have been pre-gaming, as they are toting a half-empty bottle of whiskey. They average four-feet, ten-inches and ninety pounds, so it doesn't take much. Dan picks up Mika and Irene in his arms just to show that he can.

People are having a great time. Everyone is taking sentimental photos together with goofy drunk grins. The lone guy from Kazakhstan comes up to me. His name is Nurbolat and he didn't speak a word of English when he got here. I still don't know how he turned up at Glacier. He is also the guy who, against his better judgment, chased a black bear up into a tree.

He says, "Heyyy, Andrew. Great party. Many people. Good time." His English has improved dramatically, and I love it. Meanwhile, the Czech and Slovakians are getting hammered. Many of them are leaving in two days, and this is their last party. They sway unsteadily back and forth and sing loudly in Czech. Then Clint and the boat crew show up.

"You think we would miss this party?" Those guys had a couple of ragers earlier in the summer at the boathouse. One had a cowboy and Indian theme, and the other was a captain's ball. People begin to leave because many of them still have to work tomorrow. I can't go anywhere because I signed a sheet for the NPS saying if there was anything on the ground the next morning, we would be in trouble and further partying would be banned. So I hang with Taiwan Nation and the Eastern Europeans until four in the morning. Dan and I stay even later to clean up. Todd asked me earlier if I was going to make it into work on time the next day, and I said "no problem," but that is not going to happen.

The bonfire is a precursor to a couple weeks of goodbyes. Since I have nothing better to do, I volunteer to take friends to the airport so that they don't have to take a shuttle. Most of them will still have a week or two in the country to travel around. The majority of them choose the West

Coast. Only one person will visit Chicago—Ane, from Germany, and she loves it.

———————

The final official activity is the employee dinner, which is for all of the people still here during the final week, so it is mostly Americans and a few international stragglers. The event turns disastrous after the dining room manager ambitiously organizes a disc golf drinking game that afternoon. He spent hundreds of dollars on booze and mapped out a whole course around the grounds, with each hole representing a different drink. He had to wait until the end of the season to orchestrate this so that there'd be no tourists walking around.

By dinnertime, most of the attendees are extremely intoxicated. People are knocking over glasses, slurring their words during speeches, and making general asses out of themselves. Afterwards, one guy smashes a window by trying to throw a ball at a guy who has passed out. What a fitting way to end the season. I give a brief speech, making fun of Todd and his southern accent and his inability to pronounce any of the international names correctly. They hand out prizes and merchandise as part of a raffle, and the dinner, as well as the summer, comes to a close.

———————

I was one of the first people to arrive and am one of the last to leave. Everything is closed for the season, so I walk around one more time and take pictures of the boarded up windows and the animal heads with dust coverings over them. I take one last look at my office and the picture of the mother grizzly with her cubs, which now has a whole new meaning for me. The creek running by the lodge has slowed to a trickle and doesn't even make it to the lake. It won't flow steadily again until the snow melts next April. I drive up the road and do the same hike I did the very first day along McDonald Creek. It looks like a normal creek now—not the raging river it was four months ago. I also hike the Avalanche Lake trail one more time. I tell Todd it was a fun season, but that I do have some feedback for him. I tell him I was doing about ten hours of actual work a week and left at three each day to go hiking, which he already knew. I tell him there just wasn't much to do and that a front desk person should do the job.

I pack my car, say goodbye to Dan, and hit the road back to the Midwest. I visit Yellowstone National Park on the way home, crash in Boulder for a night, and make it back to central Iowa in early October, wondering what to do next.

# MAIL ROOM FOR IMPROVEMENT

It's 10:40 p.m. on a Wednesday night. I start to pack up my stuff and change out of my sweaty gear.

"Where are you going? We have the gym for another hour," says a fellow ultimate player.

"I have to get to work. I start at 11:00," I reply.

"Have fun with that."

I walk out into the frigid January air, warm up my car, and hit the road. I arrive just before my shift starts. As I walk up to the building, the guy that works with me on my line finishes his cigarette and grumbles sarcastically like he does every night, "We having fun yet?"

"Always," I say.

The night crew assembles in the break room. Some people are eating last minute snacks and others are cramming in a few minutes of shut-eye before the shift begins. Most of us are drinking either coffee or soda. At 11:00 sharp, we head to the "lines."

It is another day—or is it night—at the mail sorting facility on the outskirts of town. The place runs 24/7, with its bright interior lights and lack of windows sealing out the real world. *This* will be our world for the next eight hours. I go to my line and as usual, the Vietnamese and Laotian women from second shift are working furiously with an unexplained zeal. They will be here for another thirty minutes. Then we will take over until our replacements arrive at 7:00 a.m.

I woke up at 4:00 p.m. today and am full of energy and dart left and right to grab pieces of mail from different slots of the machine, putting them into the corresponding boxes. I was trained in two minutes for this job. There were no explanations given on my first day or at any time afterwards. Walk around, take mail out of the machine, and put it in a box. That is it. Don't ask what the numbers mean, where the mail is going, how much needs to be done, why they need temp employees, or anything else. Just sort.

The night shift boss walks by. He could be thirty years old or sixty-five—I really can't tell. He has some grey hair on a balding head paired with a young face and blue eyes. I have spoken with him once. The temps just show up, move around, and then take off. In the break room before our shift, rumors of a short shift float around.

"I heard we'll get out really early tonight. There's hardly any mail."

"I heard that too."

We will find out in eight hours that these rumors are not true. People say this every day, but more often than not we don't roll out of here until 7:30. It's like an annual parole hearing, where there is hope that *this* time we will get out of the slammer, but then are told, "Not yet. Maybe next year."

The Asian women depart. Now we're on our own.

"Bye. Have a good night . . . day . . . whatever it is," they say.

I mindlessly sort and look across to the other lines. I am three weeks into this two-month assignment, but only recognize a couple of workers. People don't last here. They don't last long at all. This job has a higher turnover rate than the Soviet forces on the Eastern Front. The other day, I trained two guys. One guy didn't show up again and the other only lasted two days. The guy that trained me disappeared after three days. I am now a seasoned veteran.

Two jobs are involved with the line: the operator and the sorter. The operator shoves thousands of pieces of mail into the machine. Our operator is the "We having fun yet?" guy. Everyone else sorts. The machine is thunderous and we scramble to keep up as mail flies all over the place.

If any one box gets too full, the machine jams, causing our operator to turn off the machine, walk to the jam, curse under his breath, and mutter, "I am not in the mood for this tonight."

He clears the machine, walks back, turns the machine on, and we resume.

Occasionally during a jam, a full-time employee will come out of his office, where he was probably playing video games, and ask us why the machine isn't on.

"It just jammed."

"Oh, okay." Images of chained slaves working on the Egyptian pyramids pass through my mind. I'm just glad that they aren't allowed to beat us with leather whips.

Another full-timer walks out from somewhere and yells, "Break time!"

All the machines fall silent as we rush away from the work floor. We have exactly fifteen minutes of freedom. A good percentage of the night crew grabs their coats and makes their way outside for a smoke break. One man walks by explaining that he is down to two packs a day. The rest of us go to the break room to sit at tables surrounded by vending machines. One guy immediately falls asleep. A few others buy soda or stare blankly at the wall. A guy from Houston explains to no one that he only listens to rock and rap because that's what he grew up on. I get out a book.

Two people talk about how their lines are doing and whether we will get off early today.

"We got a lot of skids left."

"Our machine keeps breaking down!"

"Will we have to sort orange tonight?"

A nineteen-year-old woman tells two others about her three kids, including her four-year-old, who likes to "talk back." The Bosnian dude cracks jokes in broken English. One woman says this is her last night. She has gotten a job doing data entry at a local bank making eleven dollars an hour—more than she has ever made in her life. Another woman asks everyone why no one was here two nights ago. She swears she was told to come in, but when she arrived, there were no cars in the parking lot and the door was locked.

People ignore her at first, but finally someone says, "We never work that night. You must have missed the memo."

Fifteen minutes are up in a heartbeat. Back into the pit. We are less than two hours away from our thirty-minute lunch break. It is now about that time when I get out my iPod to give myself a boost.

While going through the mail to check for barcodes, a guy working on the adjacent line and I will occasionally find interesting names that we show each other—a small game to break the monotony. I show him a guy in Texas named Ben Loser, and later he comes back with a guy in California named Luke Gentleman. We go through tens of thousands of letters every night, so this game never gets old.

A woman I trained a few days ago walks by and I hope she doesn't talk to me. She had told me she was in business school, although after a troubling incident yesterday, I have to wonder. We were getting out early since it was a holiday, and were told to finish up and head out after just two hours.

She came over and said, "If we leave early, what do we put down on the timesheet?"

"I would imagine we put down that we worked two hours," I replied.

"Oh. We don't put down eight hours?"

"I don't . . . think so. Since we only worked two hours, we should probably put down two hours."

"But I already wrote down eight hours when I signed in," she said.

"Hmmmmm. I think that might be a little suspicious. Generally, since we don't know when we will be done, you just sign in and then you sign out whenever you leave. You can probably just scratch out what you wrote and put down two hours." She looked really confused, but I continued, "If everyone put eight hours instead of two, they might notice. It's kind of lying and immoral."

I didn't seem to have convinced her. This is the same woman who showed up alone a couple nights ago. Tonight, she says she would love to go home early because she had twisted her ankle wrestling with her husband. I avoid eye contact with her and slowly drift to a different part of the machine.

It's 3:00 a.m. Lunchtime. The first four hours generally go by fairly quickly. People get out their sandwiches or warm up leftovers they brought from home. Some people trek to the "Always Open" Subway down the street. I use the time to read and utilize my brain since that is not an option while I work. The energy level has dropped since the first break. People are zoning out as we head into the second half of the night shift. After reading for most of the break, I decide to go outside for a minute or two. A blast of sub zero air is the best way to wake up. It is pitch black out and ridiculously cold. Ten people are smoking and shivering furiously. One man mentions that he just paid ninety dollars to fill up his Suburban and I head back indoors.

The thirty-minute lunch break goes by faster than a car at the Indy 500 track. It is a phenomenon all of us are still trying to figure out: How can thirty minutes on the line feel like three hours, while our lunch feels like thirty seconds? We have to wake up a couple people who have fallen into deep sleep. This is very considerate of us, because if you fall asleep you might be fired. At least that's why I am here. I replaced a guy that fell asleep in the bathroom a few weeks ago. Even though we don't know each other's names, keeping people from losing their jobs seems like the right thing to do. Most people wouldn't be here if they had better options, so we have to look out for each other.

Now begins the shortest segment of the shift, from 3:30 to 5:00. We are rejuvenated from food and only have ninety minutes to slog through until the final break. We have a better idea of our progress with the pallets. As we sort, I look over and admire the sight of the dwindling pallets. I glance over to the wall and see that there are no pallets left.

*Maybe we will get out early tonight after all.*

Suddenly, as if out of thin air, a guy appears, hauling a giant, bulging pallet, and says, "Here you go." My heart sinks. We are going to be here all night.

There must be some magical place in the warehouse that I haven't discovered where they hoard pallets to bring out at the last second so we can be fooled into keeping up good spirits in hopes of finishing early. Like clockwork, they will bring out more mail at 5:30, and we are defeated. This is also around the time of night when I turn my iPod on full blast with upbeat songs. I start to sing out loud—anything to pass the time faster.

We take our final break, which goes by in a nanosecond, and go back to the line for the last two hours, which lasts longer than the first six hours. I find myself glancing up at the clock.

5:27.

I look up twenty minutes later.

5:30.

Oh. My. God. It's like a bad trip where time no longer exists. The bright lights start to take their toll. Everyone morphs into zombies with bloodshot eyes. Nobody speaks. We sort. We just sort. We silently applaud when the machine jams—a free mini-break. I pace around so I don't collapse. I see a piece of mail to be sent to a Jon Cleavige and show it to my coworker. We share a smile and then start sorting again.

It is 7:00 a.m. The morning shift workers descend like a squadron of backup troops. We have held the fort all night, but casualties have been mounting and we are fading fast. These people have just woken up and are ready for action. They start grabbing mail left and right, putting boxes here and there. We are saved.

We do almost no work for the final thirty minutes because we have nothing left. The Mexican woman who takes over our line starts barking at us, saying she likes a clean line and everything prepped. She starts putting everything where she wants it. We don't hear anything she says—we don't care. It's 7:20. That's good enough for me; I go to the office to sign out and everyone follows suit. We shuffle out of the building as the sun comes up. I warm up the car and then head straight into rush hour traffic, except I'm not going to work, but to bed. I will wake up in the afternoon to do it all over again. And, there is a part of me that is curious to see who else will be willing to show up for one more day.

# MAIL IN THE COFFIN

I take a stack of documents over to the president of a small insurance company.

"All done."

"Thanks, and that's it. Looks like we don't have any work left. You worked too fast." I nod, thank her, and leave the building.

Two weeks ago, I left my soul-draining job working as a mail sorter and came straight to this place after getting hooked up by a family friend working at a staffing agency. Higher pay, a nice downtown location in Des Moines, and regular hours. I especially enjoyed my lunch breaks, during which I would walk around exploring the city's famed skywalk system, one of the largest in the world. I could walk a couple miles through the maze-like pedways without ever stepping out into the frigid air. I wove through droves of women power-walking on their lunch breaks and gazed at the few people down below shivering their asses off.

The work was easy, but evidently I was too efficient for my own good, because what was supposed to be a month-long gig wrapped up in two weeks.

I call the friend and he says he's sorry that the company flaked out but that he can get me another job back at the mail place—but this time, the day shift, which is 7:00 a.m. to 3:30 p.m. I don't really have a choice, so I accept.

The next day, I find myself back at the mail warehouse and a sense of dread washes over me. I feel like a guy that has waited in line forever only to turn a corner to see that the line stretches for miles in a new direction.

Even though it is just two weeks later, I don't recognize a single person, except the full-time staff that never seems to do anything. I head back to my old line and meet my new crew. We have a new operator. Apparently the "We having fun yet?" guy was fired for telling the warehouse manager to fuck off. Everyone reaches his or her limit at this place sooner or later.

On my line are three Spanish-speaking people: one older Mexican woman who never says a word and two friends—one El Salvadoran and one Mexican. They say their names are Neil and Ted.

*Riiiiiigggggghhhht.*

And my name is Feliciano Eduardo Almagro, a three-star shortstop prospect whose batting average wasn't cutting it, so here I am. Whatever it takes to get through the staffing agency paperwork. They are nice guys and immediately begin teaching me Mexican slang. We proceed to refer to ourselves as "huey" throughout the day. This is like calling someone an "asshole," but a little friendlier.

My look-for-funny-names-on-letters partner is now a full-time maintenance guy. No one else looks familiar. Several middle-aged women complain about the job because they were making much more from unemployment than from this gig. Then there are two girls that must be about eighteen. They never leave each other, and they don't do anything. Halfway through the day, when I go to the office to ask a question, they are in there and have been for hours, flirting with one of the full-timers. When they are out on the line, they are operators and don't sort any mail.

*Who are these girls?*

When the machine breaks down, they just sit down on a pallet and hang out until someone else figures out the problem. The worst part is that they boss everyone around and people actually do what they say because of the girls' connection to the full-timers.

During a break one day, I go over to talk to a cute woman who always comes in at four in the morning and works until noon. I first saw her when she was working the night shift and now I see her in the early part of my shift. I had finally gotten the courage to talk to her a few days ago. She told me that she moved to Des Moines from Cambodia and is now working odd hours making shipping labels. I told her I would burn a CD mix for her since she occasionally listens to music during work. I walk over and give her the CD.

"Thanks. You didn't need to do that. I will listen to it on the way to Cambodia in a couple weeks."

"Nice. You're going to Cambodia. Visiting family?"

"Yeah, me and my husband are going to visit some relatives for the first time in a while."

*Your husband. Dammit.*

"Well, that sounds awesome. Hope you enjoy the trip and the music."

I slink back to the line. You can't win if you don't play the game, but there is no victory in this place.

A couple weeks later, an amazing thing happens. A guy walks in, and I find out that I have something in common with him. He knows what is going on in the world, hates this place as much as I do, and is in to mixed martial arts. In fact, he may be the biggest MMA fan in the world. I rack my brain to come up with obscure fighters that fought years ago, and he knows everything about them. He is a bigger MMA fan than I am a tennis fan, and that's saying a lot. We work on different lines, but we are able to talk through the racks about sports and newsworthy events. Like me, he immediately notices the two snotty girls, and we both decide that we won't listen to anything they say.

Later on, as if on cue, one of the girls tells us to leave line six and go to line one.

"Um, no thanks. We're good here."

She glares at us.

"Yep," I continue. "Line six, that's really my scene, you know? Home away from home. Not really feeling line one today."

There is nothing she can do because she is nothing. She only has power because people think she has power, but now that we have challenged it, it's clear that her reign of terror has ended for those of us that will defy her.

Later on, something doesn't seem right. I look at the zip code being printed on all of the letters from the current pallet, and notice that nothing is correct. I alert our operator who relays the message to the supervisor. Five minutes later he is barking for people from all of the lines to come over to our line where we spend the next hour taking out thousands of pieces of mail from hundreds of boxes and putting a blank label on them. It is about as efficient as mowing the lawn with nail clippers. But it could have been worse. If the mistake were not found, we would have sent tens of thousands of pieces of junk mail into a black hole. OH! NO! Maybe I shouldn't have said anything. Still, even a different mindless activity is better than working the line.

Early one Friday, I look up and see—it can't be . . . shit. It is the guy from the previous staffing agency who got me the night shift at this place. I dart around the machine and hope he doesn't spot me. I don't know why I don't want him to see me, but it seems like the best option. He glances over at my line and I think I'm done for. I look down and pretend to do something. I walk slowly away in the opposite direction and he leaves a couple minutes later. Bullet dodged.

Not quite. Moments after getting home I get a call from a random Des Moines number. I make the mistake of picking up.

"Andrew, it's John. That was you at the mail place today, right?"

The correct answer is no.

"Yeah . . . what's up?"

"I thought so. Yeah . . . yeah . . . we don't DO that, kay!"

"Do what?"

"I got you a gig at that place and you don't just go around my back and go through some other temp agency, you understand!"

Is he going to kill me?

"Well, I had quit to do this other gig that didn't work out, but the guy that got me that gig was able to get me back on this one. I didn't know the code of conduct for working with temp agencies."

"It's just a lack of respect. I get you a job, and you bail like that. That's just unacceptable. It's unprofessional."

We are on completely different pages. I do realize that he gets paid commissions for placing people, but last time he got me a job, I was working with a bunch of zombies and eventually turned into one myself.

"This other guy offered me a day shift, so I figured I would take it. It didn't cross my mind to call you again since I had left the place and thought I was a done deal at your staffing place."

John snaps that I have a lot to learn, and hangs up. I really hope I don't see him at the warehouse again.

During the day shift there are some projects at the warehouse that involve a tiny amount of thinking, which could not be said about the night shift duties. For instance, we break down pallets into more specific boxes for the local mail. We also help prep the shipping containers by moving the finished boxes to the right areas. Previously, much of the warehouse was dark with only the mail sorting area lit. Now I see that the place is huge, with tons of people working on machines that seem to have emerged straight from a science fiction movie. There are conveyor belts bringing boxes to where they are crushed, machines with pistons going up and down, and many others that I stay far away from so that I don't lose a limb.

Often times, all of the mail being shoved into the machine is for one zip code, which means that the letters will all come out of one slot. This also means that the other people need to recognize this and come over to help. One person takes the mail out using the proper technique so that the envelopes don't erupt all over the place. The second person takes the stacks and puts them into a box, and the third person preps more boxes and does labeling. But there is trouble on my line. My Spanish-speaking brethren are good guys, but they are huge slackers. I consider myself a huge proponent of efficient work methods, but these guys have taken slacking to a whole new extreme. When one person is forced to take on three people's tasks alone, things go to shit quickly.

For a while, I do it all because I can. But then I get pissed. Fifteen feet from me, three people are hanging out, oblivious to the world, so I stop working. Within seconds, the machine jams and turns itself off. Everyone looks up, annoyed—what are you doing? They gradually come over and help clean out the machine and pick up pieces of mail off the floor. I politely explain that it is a mindless job but that you have to put forth at least a *little* effort to help out when situations like this occur. The jam takes several minutes to clean up, and everyone makes it look like my fault, but I feel like I need to teach the new people a lesson about team-work before I am gone.

Among the many differences between the day and night shifts is the fact that I have an end date in mind. I have committed to travel to Miami to volunteer at a major tennis tournament. I was let go as a high school tutor a few weeks ago, so I don't have that to worry about anymore. It was a brutal ritual. I would get off at 7:30 in the morning, go out to breakfast, drink a bunch of coffee, and head to the tutoring place, where I taught kids geometry, algebra, and scientific reasoning skills for the ACT. My mind wasn't really there so I was released from my duties.

Working without an end date here is like being stranded on an island and not knowing if help will ever come. Giving myself a last day to look forward to puts a ship on the horizon, and my release from purgatory is in sight. I still have to get through a few more days, but then that will be it.

The last day is here, and for some reason I am working harder than ever. I close my eyes and imagine the beaches of Key Biscayne.

*Just get through this. Only a couple more hours.*

I look around at all of the things I hope never to see again. The drab break room. All of the lines to which I have been shackled like a gal-ley slave. The people that come and go. And it's time. I am the first one to clock out. I go talk to the head boss who has no idea who I am, even though I have worked here longer than anyone.

"Yeah, so it's my last day. Here's my security card."

I turn around and leave. I feel like a falsely convicted man getting out of prison after being exonerated with new DNA evidence. As I pull out of the parking lot, life has meaning again.

# LOSING MY CENSUS OF REALITY

I am watching Andy Murray, the fourth-best tennis player in the world, play some chump on center court at the Sony Ericsson Open in Miami. I have the best seat in the house—right on the court and I didn't pay a dime. I am volunteering for the second straight year and am on the "safety" team. I sit next to the main court entrances and make sure that only people with the proper credentials get in. This includes on-court staff, coaches, photographers, family members, and significant others. For the early matches there aren't a lot of people in these areas, so I get to watch world-class tennis for a couple hours before I am moved to a different post.

I get a phone call and take it in a hallway inside the stadium.

"Hi, it's Earl from the Census Bureau in Des Moines. You applied a year ago to be a census enumerator, and we finally have dates for training. Are you still available?" The timing is perfect so I accept the offer. I volunteer the rest of the week in Miami, spend a couple of days in Detroit visiting my buddy Dan from Glacier, and get back to Des Moines just in time for training.

---

In Singapore and other advanced countries, the census is done completely online because everyone has Internet access. For the 2010 United States Census, the government will employ millions of enumerators to canvass every neighborhood in the country in order to follow up with households that never sent in their paper questionnaires. The Founding

Fathers established a mandate that requires the population to be counted every ten years in order to determine the ratio of congressional representatives. This year, the grim economic outlook has caused an outcry for the reevaluation of this ritual, which will take over a year to complete and cost billions of dollars. Russia was one of the countries that scrapped its census because it determined that it wasn't worth the cost.

Ultimately, this year's census will proceed just like the previous ones but with a small change. The majority of households will receive a condensed version with just ten basic questions. A small percentage of households will receive a longer form that asks about occupation, salary, and other specific information. Participation is apparently mandatory, although we're never told what happens if people refuse to oblige.

---

On the scheduled day, I show up for training at a church in West Des Moines. There are twelve of us and I am the youngest person in the room by thirty years. A few of these people have worked one or two previous censuses. Our crew leader is a woman named Veronica who has taken an indefinite leave from her job as an attorney. She will walk us through a week of training. Our first task is to go to the kitchen and register our fingerprints. Then we review the extraordinary amount of paperwork we must complete to be authorized for the myriad tasks involved with this gig. We have to fill out a sheet of paper for every day we do any work. We have to include our name, employee ID number, task code, office code, the date, hours worked, the operation name, our points of travel, and about ten other pieces of information. This is standard protocol even if we only work for an hour. After it takes nearly two hours to go over the pay form, I can tell it's going to be a long week.

We also have to fill out a dozen forms for payroll and for general employee information. I begin to realize why our government never accomplishes anything. Some laws take years to come about. This is why. We go on our break halfway through the day, and we haven't even discussed the 2010 Census. When we get back, Veronica explains that we will be working on the enumeration phase of the census, which is the meat of the operation. Several months ago, locators walked around neighborhoods all over the country and mapped out every household address, a task Google Earth probably could have done in a matter of seconds. They sent out forms to all of those households three weeks ago, and most people returned them voluntarily. Our job is to follow up on all of the forms that were not returned.

It turns out that our job won't take long at all because the upper Midwest, including Iowa, along with Minnesota and Wisconsin, had a return rate significantly higher than the rest of the country. This makes sense because people in the Midwest generally do things they are supposed to do, no questions asked. It is a different world in this part of the country. Strangers say hello with regularity. People hold doors open. People come to complete stops at stop signs. And they return their census forms as soon as they get them because it's the right thing to do.

My parents received the long version of the questionnaire and finished it by the next day.

"Andrew, put your information in here now. We need to get this out tomorrow morning."

Approximately eighty percent of Iowans returned their forms and in West Des Moines the return rate was even higher. This means we might only be out in the field for two or three weeks, while our counterparts in California and Texas will be working for months.

When we finally start to learn about the census form, it becomes clear that it is mind-numbingly simple, and it infuriates me that people can't be bothered to take three minutes to fill it out and send it back. The first part asks how many people live in the house. Then it goes on to ask for names, relations, birth dates, race, and whether they rent or own their house. That's it.

We spend thirty hours over the next four days going over this form. We role-play as household members and interviewers. If things stay simple and the person is cooperative, it takes about five minutes. There are many ways for things to get complicated though. People can have ten kids, which requires a supplemental form as well as all of the names of the children. There are college students living in dorms during the school year, military personnel shuttling between bases, kids of divorced parents living in two homes—the list of tricky scenarios is endless, but we are told not to worry about these because they rarely come up.

Finally, it's time for the real deal. We are given our official binders, which include all of the forms for the missing households as well as detailed maps of the area. Each binder has about forty residences. We can work whenever we want, but at reasonable hours, as in times when we can actually find people at home. If we go at 8:00 a.m. on a Tuesday and no one is there, we shouldn't go at 8:00 a.m. on the following day. Midday is good for catching stay-at-home people and retirees, who supply us with lemonade, cookies, and bland conversation. Early evenings and weekends are good for catching the rest of the population.

We are told to work our first day in pairs to ease into the process. My partner and I agree to go to a random neighborhood. Lo and behold, occupants of the first residence are home and invite us in. It is like a virtual simulation of the ideal interview. They are retirees who had been in Florida for the winter and their census form was lost in the shuffle. After verifying that they did not fill out a form in Florida, we are able to go through the questionnaire just like we practiced. Easy as pie. After doing two more together, we agree that we are ready to go solo.

There is no time limit or itinerary set for us. A couple people are working other jobs and have time constraints as to when they can go out. But, the rest of us can start right away. It is going to be a competition of sorts, because we have been told that there are only twenty-five binders in total, which means two binders per person on average. As soon as someone finishes a binder, they move on to another one. If you start off slacking, someone might end up taking work from you. As a result, most people begin hitting the streets immediately.

Seventy-five percent of my time is spent driving to different neighborhoods trying to locate the correct houses. I learn the proper way to read the maps and take the most efficient routes to houses without backtracking. Most people aren't home, so we leave a sheet of paper on the door saying we had stopped by. They can call the number provided to complete the form over the phone or they can wait for us to return. The majority of people are friendly, but a lot of them did not return their forms for a reason. For the most part, they think the census is dumb and a waste of their time.

Or, they believe that there is a massive government conspiracy to steal their identities and ruin their lives, like one guy I come across half-way through the week.

I ring the bell. A man cracks the door open, peers around, and sees me wearing my United States Census messenger bag, wielding a clipboard.

"What do you want?"

"Hello sir, my name is Andrew Edwards and I'm with the US Census Bureau. Is this 7988 Musa Street?"

"Why do you want to know?"

"Well, sir, we are conducting the 2010 Census. Every ten years, since 1790, we count the population of the country."

"You guys just want to steal my information."

"Sir, we aren't stealing anything. We do this in order to know the correct ratio of representatives in Congress. Not to mention local funding is based on how many people live in a certain area. If everyone isn't counted, our community won't be accurately represented, and we won't get as much funding for roads, hospitals, and schools."

"No, no, no. I'm not going to do anything with this."

"Sir, the census form this year is the simplest, shortest, and most streamlined form in the history of the survey. We ask how many people live here, birth dates, male or female, and that's it. Five minutes. Piece of cake."

My off-script appeal goes unheeded.

"Why are you bothering me in my home! You guys send me stuff, and now you're at my home! Why are you picking on me!" His voice quavers as his agitation mounts.

"Sir, everyone in the country is sent a form because the same people that created this country thought it was important to know how many people live in the country."

"I'm not giving out anything to you people. Leave me alone!" He slams the door in my face.

Now we're talking. No more grandmas politely offering me tea and telling me stories while doing the questionnaire. This guy was the highlight of the job so far, but what's going to be awkward for both of us is that I will have to stop by his house again as dictated by protocol. I can't wait for that next attempt.

Other residents are very coy in their refusal. They spend more time explaining why they don't need to fill out the form than it would take to actually do it. I want to tell them how fucking stupid they are and that they are wasting my time, but in training we were taught to remain professional and to politely explain the importance of our work. If people adamantly refuse after several attempts, or get violent, we can give up and let another crew deal with it in a later phase.

———————

I finish my first binder in less than a week and meet with Veronica in a coffee shop to check my progress. I show her the completed forms and explain the tricky situations, which includes the encounter with the paranoid guy. Unfortunately, he was not around on my two other attempts so someone in a later phase will have to track him down. Everything is tiptop and she says I have been incredibly efficient in terms of the time I have put down and the amount of surveys I have completed. This is because I am a fast walker and can quickly make my way between houses. In college, I got a reputation for speed walking to places. In fact, someone came up with a term for it—Edwardian Pace—and the term is still in use today. It often causes problems when I stop paying attention and find myself way ahead of the group. Now, the Edwardian Pace is causing another dilemma—the faster I go, the quicker I will be out of a job. Oh well, that's what happens when you only have eighty houses to do because everyone already dutifully sent in their forms.

My second binder contains only apartments, which means I can park and go through all of the households in one stop. In theory this should be quick, but the apartment manager is not playing team ball and refuses to tell me which apartments are vacant now and which ones were vacant on

April 1st. So I go through the big complex with forty forms and only two people are home. For all I know, thirty of these places are vacant, but since the woman in the front office won't help me, I return to this place several times and never get a hold of anyone.

I am not a certified Spanish interviewer, but I do come across a few apartments with Latinos and decide I will have a go at it. There is a Spanish form, which I lost, so I have to translate the English version in my head and ad-lib it. I manage to do it successfully and am pleased that my rapidly disintegrating Spanish skills I had honed in Costa Rica are still worth something.

Walking around putting forms on doors is dull work, but it is better than sitting at a desk. I deal with a few more crazies who think their lives will be ruined if they divulge their gender or birth date, but since this is Iowa, most people politely comply and thank me for performing a valuable civic service. I spend about as much time filling out my pay sheets as I do in the field. We are told that we can count the time we spend filling out pay forms. We are also compensated for mileage and the time we spend in transit. People that live in the country can make bank spending hours driving hundreds of miles to isolated residences.

---

The job is over after three weeks. I look at my last pay stub to see that I spent the same amount of time working in the field as in training. Why do Iowans have to be so diligent in turning in government-related things? On the bright side, if I am free in May 2020, I will have a leg up with experience and could get a position for that census. Unless we finally catch up to Singapore and are able to have machines do these things for us. But I wouldn't count on it.

# BAD STATE OF A FAIR

I receive a call from a guy in New York who works at Lead Wolf Marketing in regards to a Craigslist ad I responded to. There is going to be a three-day event at the Iowa State Fair promoting AARP Magazine. It is a nationwide tour, mainly targeting state fairs, and they need locals at each site to work the events. The brand ambassadors must be full of energy and love working on their feet. They must be able to smile and engage strangers, along with a bunch of other bullshit. I give him the answers he wants to hear, and I get the job. Shortly after, I receive an email with way too much information about AARP, directions to the fair, and the dress code. I don't bother to read it, and instead relax, because I am scheduled for more than thirteen hours each day for the next three days.

———————

On the morning of the first day, I don the required khaki pants and regret this immediately when I step outside. It is already eighty degrees and as sticky as gum on hot pavement. As usual, I arrive early and park in an East Des Moines neighborhood. The sidewalk is littered with trash from fairgoers the previous night. The only people I see are elderly attendees who have woken up early in order to be the first ones through the gate. Maybe there is an early bird special at the Butter Cow[3]. It appears that we are already missing potential visitors to the AARP tent.

———

3 The Butter Cow is the top attraction at the Iowa State Fair. It is a full-sized replica of a cow made completely of butter.

I wait for ten minutes at the designated gate, and decide to call the contact number for the boss on site. No one picks up. We're off to a good start. I start to worry that I am at the wrong gate, so I walk around to another one. I can't go in without paying—we had been told that the tour managers would meet us at the gate on the first day to outfit us with credentials. I don't bother trying to explain to the gatekeepers that I am an employee like them. Five minutes later, a few more people in khakis amble up, and we wait together. Eventually, a man and woman walk towards us and introduce themselves. They are Anthony and Michelle, our supervisors for this event. They have been doing this for several months all over the country and this is their penultimate fair—the Minnesota State Fair will be their next and final destination.

We go to the tent and are given bright orange AARP Magazine T-shirts, an item that I will donate to Goodwill a few days later. This is our uniform for the next three days. Less than thirty minutes after I put it on, it is completely drenched in sweat.

We go through introductions and get to know the team. There are seven brand ambassadors (desperate out-of-work people in AARP shirts) in addition to our supervisors. There are two guys; the rest are women and most of them are pretty cute. This is no accident because when you apply to these kinds of jobs, most companies require headshots along with your résumé. Two of the women are a mother and daughter combo that worked here last year. Besides the mom, I am the oldest person on the team. One of the girls is in school and models on the side. The other guy is back living at home after graduating college in Michigan. Everyone stumbled upon this gig like I did.

Our supervisors, Anthony and Michelle, are from California and New York City, respectively. They don't seem thrilled to be in Iowa. They seem miffed by the sight of the huge tractors nearby and the farmers walking around in overalls.

The first order of business is to set up the area. The main tent is up, but now we need to finish everything else, including unloading all the "goodies." For those that haven't attended the Iowa State Fair, the number one activity for visitors is collecting freebies from every possible tent on the grounds. These items include information fliers, pencils, key chains, mini-flashlights, nail clippers, letter openers, and every other kind of flimsy trinket imaginable.

My dad is one of the worst culprits of this "sport." He collects enough stuff each year to fill a drawer and then won't touch the things for years. His enjoyment stems from getting the merchandise rather than actually using it. He has a huge collection of letter openers.

"You can never have enough," he says. Yardsticks, cheap paper fans, magnets—the stuff of a collector's wet dream. Hopefully this behavior isn't hereditary.

State fair employees have already deposited over a hundred unmarked boxes containing all of the goodies we need for the event. We will be promoting a new beverage, Benevia, as well as giving away healthy snacks. There are also dozens of different fliers promoting travel to Wyoming and Idaho, as well as pamphlets hawking reduced car insurance and various programs targeting people over the age of fifty-five. Then, I come across the item that will nearly cause a stampede later—a medium-size 2011 edition of the United States Rand McNally road atlas. If there is one thing everyone will take, it is a road atlas.

The rest of the boxes contain the Spin-to-Win prizes. Hand-powered flashlights, mini-radio headsets, stress balls, books, pads of paper, and pocket calculators. It takes us an hour to unload the goods and set up the tables, the Spin-to-Win wheel, and a big board to be used for an undisclosed purpose. At this point, Michelle decides that it is go-time and begins to delegate positions. Maybe she got bored of texting on her phone while Anthony and the rest of us were sweating our asses off. She says we will start with different positions and rotate periodically.

"You, what's your name again?" she asks me.

"Andrew."

"Why don't you work the Dream Board to start off? I'll come over in a little bit to explain how it works." I walk over to the big board we had set up earlier. There is zero shade here, and it is now over ninety degrees. I have a bad feeling about this. Michelle comes over and explains how this exciting post will work. There is a small table with big post-it notes and markers. This is the Dream Board, where people will write their dreams on a card, and I will put them on the board. It is my job to fill this gigantic board with dreams. My task is to ask people: If nothing was holding you back—money, time, kids, anything—what would you do?

"People have to know that even though they are over fifty-five, they can still have dreams," Michelle says.

I glance over and see twenty people in line for the Spin-to-Win. I don't think this is going to be a very popular stop on the AARP Roadshow. I hate this already.

"Sounds like fun," I tell her. She turns around and goes back to the tent and glues herself to her phone once more.

A few people walk by. "It's the Wall of Dreams, guys! What is your dream?" People either look annoyed or confused as they walk past me, shaking their heads. Okay. I am going to have to change tactics. I walk up to people, marker and note in hand, and give my spiel again. People are still not impressed.

"What are they giving away under the tent?" they ask.

I receive a text message. It is my parents—they have just arrived at the fair with my aunt and uncle. I discreetly reply that they need to make their way over to the tractor section and find me. A few minutes later they are here, and I pretend they are strangers. I tell them what the deal is and get them all to write a dream. Start an orphanage. Travel to a new country. Catch a huge fish. I post them on the board and space them out so that it will take fewer notes to fill the whole thing. Then I tell them they certainly have more than one dream and browbeat my mom into doing another card. I look over to see if Michelle is noticing my good work interacting with fair patrons, but she is looking at her phone. My dad shoots off to get the atlas, and then my mom says they have to go. I ask them to tell my other aunt and uncle that live in Des Moines to stop by when they get to the fair.

My dad walks back with two atlases. "You should always have a couple, just in case."

They leave, and Michelle, who has done zero work during the first two hours of the gig, does a walk around. She makes her way to the Dream Board, where I have scraped together about seven dreams, with space for a hundred more. She tells me I need to be more aggressive—that we need to *fill* this board with dreams so that we can take a picture of it. She grabs a card and gets in someone's face and tells her to write down a dream. The scared passerby scribbles something, and I post it.

"See," she says. "You need to be more proactive." She returns to the tent.

Thirty minutes later, it is finally time to switch tasks. With my shirt soaked in sweat, I move to tent duty. There is a line out to the sidewalk that will never disappear for the next three days. People want—no—*must* get free stuff. We are offering samples of healthy cereals and are constantly opening more boxes and portioning samples into little plastic cups. Then people grab a bottle of Benevia and move on to another tent. This post is a million times better than the Dream Board. People don't care what we are promoting. They just want food, drinks, and a bag of goodies they will never look at again. We are ordered to ration the atlases or we will be out in a few hours. Word has gotten out around the fairgrounds that this invaluable navigational tool is being given away next to the tractors, and droves of people are thundering towards our tent. I haven't mentioned one thing about the magazine we are supposed to be promoting. I don't care, and no one else seems to either. We are giving away AARP bags containing the latest issue, which works for me.

It's nice to be in the shade. I talk to a wacky massage therapist who has set up shop right behind us. He may or may not be part of our promotion, and is giving twenty-minute massages for free. He is very talkative and time goes faster listening to him go on about different techniques he uses.

I have also decided to work as a courier, going back behind the area to reload everybody with more freebies. The giveaways are going faster than canned food before a huge storm. They are going faster than Tiger Woods' endorsements after jilting his wife. They are going faster than tequila shots on Cinco de Mayo. You get the idea. There are times when I walk back and forth constantly, opening up new boxes to keep up with the insatiable appetite of the fairgoers. Although this work is more tiring and I get sweatier, it is much more up my alley. Contrary to what

I told the recruiter from Lead Wolf Marketing, I don't like soliciting strangers to sign up for things or to try new products. I like to remain behind the scenes and stay out of the way. I don't want to be responsible for giving away useless junk to people who will turn up on an episode of *Hoarders*.

Too soon, my time at this post has come to an end, and I must go back to engaging people again. I work the technology station with the other guy, and I quickly find it to be mind-boggling. We have three jobs. First, we politely encourage people to sign up to win a trip to South Carolina that I privately think is bogus. By doing this, AARP will procure their email addresses and probably flood them with information they have no desire to receive. Someone has ingeniously set up poles to move the Spin-to-Win line right by the technology station, so it is the next logical stop. We corral them like cattle towards the computers.

"You could win a trip to South Carolina. Sign up now!"

I don't know if this is better or worse than the Dream Board, but if I stay close enough to the computers, I can share a little shade with the machines.

The second task is to teach the elderly how to text message. This has already been a huge flop, fortunately. They have connected a giant screen to a cell phone, and we bring in people that have never sent a text message before. We show them how to type a message on their phone, and then the message appears on the board. In theory, our eager participants are supposed to write that they are having a great time at the Iowa State Fair and learning how to text at the AARP Magazine Roadshow. The screen is having trouble, so Anthony says we can nix it, which I am thankful for. That concept never had a chance: Let's use technology to teach technology to people that don't want anything to do with technology.

There is a third and similar activity at the technology hub—the e-postcard station. Like the text messaging, people can write a message on the keyboard that will go on an e-postcard they can email to others. There is a picture of the AARP tent in the background of the e-card. Surprisingly, despite the worthlessness of this activity, a handful of people do take part. The problem is, most people don't know email addresses off the top of their heads—a detail the organizers of this shindig overlooked. It's sort of like how nobody knows cell phone numbers by heart anymore because they don't have to. Some people write a message, and are stuck because they don't know any email addresses by heart.

A few others ask me, "Aren't I just sending an email to someone? What is the point of this?"

*I couldn't agree more.*

"Oh, well this is an e-card," I explain. "It's special and has an image of the fair." People aren't convinced. The technology station is not a good scene and the time drags as I anxiously wait to get moved somewhere else.

Michelle comes up to me.

*Uh oh. What did I do now?*

"Okay, you can take your twenty minute break."

Finally. I get out of there immediately. I don't know where I am headed, but I know that I need to get away from the AARP tent. I look around at the food offerings. Fried Oreos, corn dogs, funnel cakes, onion rings, ice cream, lemonade. I look for something remotely healthy. Deep-fried Spam curds, fried Snicker bars, curly fries. I settle on a small box of watermelon slices that costs more than a huge bucket of fried chicken. I also eat a pork sandwich, and then my time is up. Shit. I walk back to the AARP tent.

I knew it was inevitable. I am now put on the Spin-to-Win, which is a two-person job. The girls I am replacing have the desperate, harried look of sailors bailing water on a sinking ship. They continue to franticly dish out the goods, as the line gets even longer.

People don't care what the prizes are. We could be giving away used lottery tickets and people would still flock here. One of us handles the wheel spinning and hands out prizes while the other maintains inventory and makes sure the supply channel is running smoothly.

Since my partner is a gregarious girl who loves people, I choose to be the prize stocker guy. There is a flaw in this wheel—even if you barely spin it, it goes around several times. If you spin it hard, the way ninety-nine percent of people do, it spins *forever*. No one ever makes the connection, so the line moves at a crawl while everyone waits for the thing to stop. It is the first day, so we have plenty of prizes. The radio headsets and flashlights are popular. We also have a few cookbooks that are considered good prizes due to their scarcity. The stress balls and side bags are not as popular. Everything is garbage, but it doesn't matter.

We tell every person to gently spin the wheel in order to save everyone time, but no one listens. They waited twenty minutes, and they'll spin it as hard as they want. Families with four or five kids will come up and want all of their children to spin so that each of them can win a prize. I couldn't care less, but you can see people get angry because it isn't fair. Spin-to-Win is supposed to be fun for everyone, but it has become competitive and stressful. People don't enjoy standing in the heat, but they have no choice if they want to get their hands on an AARP notepad.

I glance over at the guy working the Dream Board, sweat patches all over his shirt. Things could certainly be worse right now. I spot my other uncle and cousin who have arrived at the fair. My uncle is one of the more ridiculous fair attendees out there. It takes about an afternoon to see everything the fair has to offer and every year the fair stays the same. My uncle will end up attending six of the ten days the fair is running, and would go more if he could. He can't get enough of it.

"The shows, exhibits, Butter Cow, super slide, diving shows, chainsaw sculptor. How could it get any better?" he asks earnestly. They come through the line, and I talk to them a little while.

Working the wheel is the second best position after working the food, drink, and atlas tent. The river of people makes the time go by quickly as I continue to open more boxes of books and balls. I am told I can take my second break and use the opportunity to bolt to the building nearby that holds the pie contests. It is air-conditioned and life is good for two minutes. I exit and navigate through the giant crowds to meet up with my cousin in the animal barn. There are hogs, cattle, and sheep everywhere, and even more people. We wander into a small structure that is housing a replica of one of the huge castles in *Lord of the Rings*. It was constructed by a guy from a small town in Iowa. It uses over 100,000 toothpicks and is perfect in every way. The man is famous worldwide for a variety of replicas and has given many of them to a museum of curiosities in Spain. Maybe his next creation will be a toothpick replica of the AARP tent with me by the Spin-to-Win wheel having a nervous breakdown.

My break is up again, and I make it back for the last third of the shift. The Dream Board is miraculously filling up. Michelle is still playing with her phone, Anthony is nowhere to be seen, and everyone is running around with boxes and giving stuff away. Michelle locks eyes with me, and I begin to dread the last few hours.

"Can you relieve Karen at the Dream Board?"

"Sure thing," I say. A couple of people are writing their dreams, smiling while they do it.

"How are you doing this?" I ask Karen in amazement.

She says she just asks people to write their dreams and they do. I want to tell Michelle that she should have the girls stay here where they are effective and I can stock the juice bottles. But I don't, and I am back at the board. I have dreams too, so I write a few down and put them up.

I want to learn to scuba dive.

I want to sail around the world.

I want to walk across the United States.

I glance around to see if Michelle is anywhere nearby. A new tactic: I tell people that if they help me fill the board, I can get out of the sun where I am getting burned. I manage to get a handful more, and the board is full. Now we can take pictures of it so that the client can see what we accomplished. Just then, the wind picks up and knocks many of the cards off the board. It begins to waver uncertainly, and I scurry out of the way. I don't want to be the guy that gets killed by a Dream Board. It eventually comes crashing down, and Anthony, who has been walking around throughout the day, sees the writing on the wall, and scraps it. Finally, things are beginning to look up.

I restock the brochures and spend as much time behind the supply tent as possible. If anyone asks, I am organizing things to streamline tomorrow's operations. We have burned through approximately one ton of stuff. I sporadically walk back and forth with boxes in my hands to appear productive. Eighty percent of the atlases are gone, but the fliers for safe driving tips remain. We put them in the free bags, so people unknowingly take them.

We have run out of ice, and people aren't happy to sip warm Benevia fruit drink, which isn't very refreshing at ninety-five degrees. Oh well, it's almost time to start the breakdown of the area. The tricky part is the Spin-to-Win wheel, where people are still lining up for free stuff. In the end, we just haul it off regardless of who is waiting, or else we would be here forever. People aren't pleased, but we don't care. The team gathers for directions on how to break everything down, and we finish in forty-five minutes.

"Great job, everyone. See you guys bright and early." We all scramble away as fast as possible. I am dead tired and can't imagine doing this for another two days, as the forecast has the next week being just as hot. Also, today is Friday, which is typically not nearly as busy as the weekend. I head home, put the AARP shirt in the washing machine, go to bed, and dream of atlases.

---

The next two days are better. There is no more Dream Board or text message screen to deal with. We run out of atlases in the middle of Saturday but still have to field questions about them until Sunday night. We have no problem getting through most of the other stuff, but we do end up with a surplus of calculators and flashlights. On Sunday, we are down to those two prizes. The wheel still shows all the prize options with no indication of our shortage.

A person lands on "radio set."

I begin my apologetic spiel. "Yeah, so, uh, you have to decide on the calculator or the flashlight."

"But it says I won a radio."

"Yeah, we don't have that anymore. Sorry." I decide to convince people to stop spinning and just grab something off the table. Hell, take two, no three. I don't care. It's a good thing Michelle went off somewhere. I have to move this merchandise and keep the line going.

On my last break, I take the sky ride. This is a gondola-like cab that carries you over the entire fairgrounds. The trip lasts about ten minutes and

I relax as I float over the meandering crowd. It is a nice way to finish this tiring gig. At the end of the day, we pack up the remnants of the site so that the movers can put it in the truck for the final leg to the Minnesota State Fair. We say our goodbyes and head our separate ways. I managed to successfully work the three days without saying a single thing about AARP Magazine. At least I was wearing the shirt. Good enough.

# THE WORLD IS MY OYSTERFEST

I haven't even started and I already regret taking this gig. I had to go downtown to fill out a bunch of paperwork at a staffing agency for a job that will last all of six hours. The trip to finish the forms, which involved a train ride there and back, took three hours. Now I am standing on a street corner waiting for the boss to arrive, getting steadily more wet in cold, drizzly weather. Six of us will be working the second shift of Roscoe Village's annual Oysterfest, one of hundreds of Chicago's street festivals. At least the commute is a breeze, since I live in the neighborhood.

The boss swings by, and explains that we will all be assigned to different gates to collect "donations" for entry into the festival. Every single street festival in Chicago has closely guarded entrances where "voluntary" contributions are demanded in the name of helping the community. Veteran festivalgoers get around this by saying they live in the neighborhood and are just trying to get home. But gatekeepers are aggressive, and don't take no for an answer. The last time I was at a street festival, I really was in my own neighborhood. When I mentioned this, the gatekeeper suggested that it was even more of a reason for me to donate because I'd see the benefits first hand. Others simply ignore the suggested donation sign and bar anyone from entering unless they cough up five or ten dollars.

Suddenly, the guy who usually avoids paying entry fees is being charged with the task of collecting them. I am assigned to the western edge of the festival, behind one of the main concert stages. I am paired with another random dude who has been working at this corner for a while, as well as an off-duty cop who is moonlighting as a security guard. The police officer is an Asian guy, about six feet two inches tall and 140 pounds, and talks about his work in the suburbs as if it is guerilla warfare in Iraq. I don't mind his absurd stories because he is actively soliciting donations, which is supposed to be my job. The other guy is cool too and shows me the ropes. We have a cashier's drawer with small bills, and a lock box, which is where we keep all of the big bills. The lock doesn't actually work, so anybody can reach in and help themselves to a wad of twenties.

My partner says the banker guy should be coming around at some point to take out cash so we don't accumulate too much. I peek in the box. There must be over $2,000 inside. Hmmmm. Having two minimum wage workers protect thousands of dollars with absolutely no oversight. Someone obviously has a lot of faith. There is no accounting system in place—no log, no pad of paper, no debits or credits. It's a vanilla operation and would make a good case study for an auditing class learning about system control flaws. It crosses my mind that taking out six or seven donations would double my pay for this six-hour shift, but I won't do it.

It amazes me how generous and lazy people are. Someone put up a huge sign saying, "$7 Suggested Donation," and it is doing all of the work for us.

People approach with money in hand.

"All right, seven dollars, out of ten. Three dollars coming back your way, sir."

"Keep it."

Someone else had figured out that people don't want to wait for change. They will give us tens and call it a day. This festival is a money-making machine. During rushes where more than ten people are waiting in line, I struggle to keep up as I sift through small bills and constantly shove more twenties into the unlocked lock box.

In the meantime, terrible bands are playing onstage next to us. A huge group of teens rush over and frantically ask us if the Neon Trees have begun their set.

"Never heard of 'em."

The bands sound particularly bad because we are located behind the stage, and the music gets distorted, turning it into garbled background noise.

Suddenly, I hear a bunch of yelling over the noise and see a trio of cops escorting a drunken dude our way.

"Fuckin', fuckin'—I'm not doing shit! What's the problem!" He slams a cup to the ground.

"Stay out of here or we'll arrest your ass," says one of the cops.

The guy eventually leaves with some friends and everything returns to normal.

Our rent-a-cop is galvanized by the incident and enters security mode. When people try to walk out with festival beer cups, he springs into action.

"Whoa, whoa, whoa guys. You're going to have to finish that in here. Can't have you fellas walking around with open containers. Just doing my job."

Some guy comes over and says I can go on break. This affords me my first chance to check out the festival since I arrived three hours ago.

This being an oyster festival, I immediately hit up the oyster tent. When I saw the listing for the gatekeeping job, I also saw ads for oyster-shuckers, which paid quite a bit more, except they only wanted experienced shuckers, and oyster-shucking is not a skill I possess. Thus, the box o' cash position. I go up to the stand and look at the menu. Okay, a half-dozen oysters—ten dollars. I'd have to forfeit nearly a quarter of today's earnings for my snack break. I decide to go hungry for the next couple hours instead.

There are several tents hawking organic products and homemade goods. The beer and wine tents are busy, as always. All of the patios at the local restaurants along the street are full of people despite the chilly weather. The rain has come and gone, so it isn't too bad. I listen to thirty seconds of an eighties cover band and turn around to head back to my post.

I start to get antsy because I have somewhere else to be, which is another reason I regret taking this gig. A buddy is having his bachelor party downtown, and I am missing the first two hours by being here and will have to haul ass to make it on time for a Second City improv comedy show.

A few minutes after returning, the "accountant" shows up to take away the haul.

"Nice work, boys. Any trouble?"

"Nope. All quiet on the Western Front. People in this 'hood enjoy donating, no questions asked."

He takes a few thousand dollars out, which is nice, because I had been getting paranoid about the unlocked box. I would constantly be looking to make sure it was still there—that some kid hadn't climbed under a fence and run off with it. Now that we have nothing but a bunch of ones and fives I can finally relax.

We do get people that ask where the money goes, a question to which we were never given an answer ourselves. In fact, all I was ever told was to come to this corner and take people's money—nothing else.

"Well, you know, there's the children's play park at Belmont and Damen and the food pantry up there on Damen. Potholes, new lights for the side streets, you name it." I enjoy making stuff up and am doing my own improv in advance of the real thing tonight.

I also enjoy the system that my partner and I have established. He is unapologetic when it comes to demanding cash from festival attendees, so he does that part. I make change and put the bills into the box. This way, I am able to avoid soliciting people, which is one activity I cannot do, unless it is for the 2010 United States Census.

The position offers a great opportunity for people watching. This is a neighborhood that has many young professionals and families, but any street festival brings a plethora of colorful characters, especially when you have big names like the Neon Trees going up on stage. Mobs of teenagers decked out in skateboard or goth attire; middle-aged guys with their receding hairlines and expanding waistlines with their arms around scantily-clad, significantly younger women; dreadlocked vegan hipsters, etc. Some people bring their own beer and sit on balconies, looking down at the crowds like at Mardis Gras. Several groups of women in their fifties enter the fest, excited to get "wild" without their husbands.

I am about ready to hit the road. It's been real. And it's certainly been fun. It just hasn't been real fun. I am done standing in one spot in cold drizzle. Finally, some random guy says we can take off. We sign a sheet at headquarters, and I run back to my apartment to change.

I make it to the Second City theatre just in time for the shit storm to hit. Our party of twenty completely wasted guys has just arrived and is attracting way too much attention. After eating giant burritos in the street, we shuffle into the theater. Some in my party go to a bar to watch the end of the Iowa football game. A couple minutes before the show begins, our bachelor bolts from the theatre. A few others follow. I find out later that he proceeded to destroy the bathroom and went to a hotel for the remainder of the night. The show begins and four others take off. I look around and see that there are only five of us left. I wave the waitress over.

"Yeah, I'll get a beer, please."

"I'm sorry sir, my manager told us that your group isn't allowed any alcoholic beverages. Apparently you are all too drunk, and we don't want you jeopardizing the show."

"I see. Well, I'm not drunk. You can trust me. I just got off work." She makes an exception for me, and I get my beer.

The show is okay, but the remnants of our group are rowdy. A couple guys are laughing at the wrong things; the performers try to keep it together as we go nuts after everything they say.

A man approaches us during intermission. "Hello. I'm the manager of Second City. Yeah, we have to ask you to leave. You guys are ruining the show."

One of the guys gets in the manager's face and says that the actors are pros and should be able to handle anything. He says that *he* is an actor, which is a complete lie, and is trained to handle tough crowds. The manager says we are messing with the vibe of the show and the crowd doesn't know when to laugh and when *not* to laugh. I try to keep cool and see both sides of the argument, but can clearly tell that we are not getting back inside, so I lead us to the bar across the street to meet the others.

Sometimes you work all day at an oyster festival and then get kicked out of a comedy club at night. Sometimes that happens.

# COKE ZERO HERO

"We've brought you here today to explain the logistics of a great campaign beginning tomorrow in the Chicago area. Coke Zero is now going to be at McDonald's, and you guys will let the public know that. I'm here with Fission Marketing. Coke hired a company that hired a company that hired us to hire you guys to help us with this project. Welcome."

I am at the Marriott on Michigan Avenue in downtown Chicago. There are thirty of us packed into a conference room being briefed on the huge promotion. McDonald's has always had Coke and it has always had Diet Coke. What does it have now? COKE ZERO. I don't know if the world is ready for this. But it's going to have to be because this campaign starts tomorrow. Only half of the promo staff is actually present; we are the team leads and will be paid a little more for being in charge of our two-person teams and we have the privilege of attending this meeting.

The guy spends an hour on an explanation that should only take five minutes: We will drive to a different McDonald's around lunch time every day for seven straight days, distribute free Coke Zero samples to customers, and inform them that Coke Zero has arrived at McDonald's. Yeah, you know, the Coke with the same great taste but zero calories. The gig couldn't be easier, the guy says. You will just be giving away free samples of a drink everyone loves.

His presentation is followed by a mundane Q and A session that includes questions about mileage reimbursements and field attire.

I am about to go home and email my partner when a woman approaches me.

"Are you Andrew? I'm your partner, Kate."

"Hello . . . I didn't think you needed to come to this meeting."

"I didn't, but I figured I would anyway so that we had another set of eyes and ears here."

*Riiiiggght.*

I find out that she doesn't have a car, but does have roller blades. She will make her way to my place tomorrow morning so we can drive together to our first McDonald's.

Later that night I glance at the email that details our specific schedule.

First up is . . . Hammond, Indiana.

Wait, what? That's fifty miles from here *and* in a different state. I look at the rest of the locations on the schedule and nearly all of them are at least twenty miles away. Between all of the teams, we will be visiting over 200 McDonald's. Yet none of the ones on my sheet are anywhere close to my apartment or my partner's. Oh well. There is no time to do anything about it. Plus, the group in charge of logistics is out of North Carolina or Georgia and probably randomized the routes without any regard for making it easier for anyone.

---

I look out the window in the morning. Kate is patiently waiting by a bus stop with her rollerblades in hand. I run outside, and we are on our way to Indiana. Kate is about forty or so and was recently laid off as a project manager of some big architectural firm. She has gone from overseeing multi-million dollar projects to handing out cans of soda. Like me, she is trying to stay active until something else comes along. It is her first gig like this and she is nervous, so she wants to do everything perfectly and by the book. I can already see an issue forthcoming.

The marketing company had explained that the gig would be from 10:30 to 2:30 each day, so that we can hit the lunch rush. 10:30 to 11:00 should be for prep, 11:00 to 2:00 for sampling, and 2:00 to 2:30 for cleanup.

In the event that we get rid of all the samples, we can leave early and still get paid for the full duration.

There is almost no traffic, and we arrive a little after 10:00 a.m. Wearing my brand new Coke Zero T-shirt, I find the manager. We are treated like royalty as she leads us into the kitchen. There is a huge tub filled with twenty cases of soda, a tray, and three hundred sampling cups. There are two large bags of ice in the freezer. We roll everything out, pour out the ice, and put the Cokes in the tub. In five minutes we are ready to go.

"Okay, I guess I'll go outside first, if that's cool," I say.

"That's fine, but we can't start yet," Kate says.

"What? Why not?"

"Because it's only 10:15. We can't start until 11:00."

*Keep your cool, Andrew. Just keep your cool.*

"I hear you. But I think that was just sort of an estimate. Since we got here early, we might as well give out samples. It would be pointless not to. The faster we get rid of them, the faster we get out of here. And we still get paid for the four hours. We got here early, so let's get to work."

"Yeah, I'm just not comfortable with that. If they came around and saw us sampling at 10:30 we could get fired."

*Wow. Come. On.*

We were told at orientation that three guys will go around late at night to set up all of the promotion locations, and that they will occasionally visit different restaurants throughout the week to make sure things are running smoothly. If they do show up to see us starting early, that would be a good thing. We would be commended for going the extra mile.

"Kate, you are welcome to sit and stare at the wall for the next forty-five minutes, but I am going to start giving out samples." I turn around and walk outside.

It is nice out, but the drive-thru is a little slow. We are on a highway with strip malls and restaurants as far as the eye can see. I have never been in this town before and probably never will be again.

I try to figure out the best way to go about this. Whenever there is a car, it zooms past me because I am a good fifteen feet from the ordering area. To really get people's attention, I will have to obstruct their path and force cars to stop, but I don't think the manager on duty is going to like that very much. I pour some samples and put them on the tray with a can of Coke Zero. Finally, someone pulls up.

"What are you giving out there?"

"Coke Zero. Now being served at McDonald's. Same great taste, minus the calories. Hit it up." I am promoting a product I will never drink myself, but attempt to smile and act the part as best I can.

"Oh, I know what it tastes like. Thought it was something new." He drives past me.

I didn't think about that. Everyone has tried this before, so why are people going to want to drink a mouthful of soda and then have a small plastic cup with Coke remnants rolling around the floor of their cars? So, I switch tactics. I walk slightly into the way of cars and force them to slow down. If one of them hits me, I may get to go home early. They roll down their windows, and I shove a sample towards them.

"Free Coke Zero samples."

They don't have time to think and just take it, and I move to another car. The faster I get these samples out, the faster I can get out of Indiana. If only Kate would be a team player. I look inside to see her looking out at me. It still isn't 11:00.

At around five til, she finally comes out and grabs a few cans and cups to take inside. Traffic begins to pick up, and I have a hard time keeping up with the cars going through the drive-thru. I haven't eaten at a McDonald's in nearly three years and don't realize how popular the place is. Billions and billions served is right. If a small town in the middle of nowhere Indiana is bustling like a fruit market in India, then the restaurant must be doing okay.

All I want to do is get rid of these cups. One of the first things addressed in the meeting yesterday was this exact issue.

"I know what y'all are thinkin'. I'm just gonna give out some samples and decide at 1:00 that that's good enough and throw away all the remainin' cups. We are going to have our guys monitorin' the stores throughout the week, so I wouldn't do that."

It is certainly tempting to throw them away, but this place is so busy that I feel we will get rid of them legitimately. Kate pops out every thirty minutes or so to grab more product.

Before we know it, we have exhausted the samples and it is only 1:30. Thankfully, Kate is fine with packing up. We empty the cooler and move it back inside.

The team that set up the operation screwed up the math to our benefit. We only needed about eight or nine cases of Coke to fill all of the sample cups, but they gave us over twenty. They did say we could take some home with us if we wanted. I don't drink soda, but my roommates do, so I take five cases, put them into the trunk, and leave the rest for the employees.

It's not fulfilling work, but it was a beautiful day to be outside and we finished early. The only shitty part was driving to a different time zone to do it. At least we get paid mileage. When we are back in Chicago, Kate grabs her roller blades from the trunk, and we agree to the same plan for the next day.

I immediately go to my computer to fill out the form that is required of the team leader for each day of the promotion. How many samples did I give away? All 300, no big deal. What were some comments from the patrons?

"This tastes exactly the same as regular Coke!"

"What a great promotion! You're such a friendly brand ambassador!"

"Thanks so much for the samples! You made my day!"

"Hey, where are the road atlases!"

That should do it. Sign, date, and submit. Then I change clothes and rush off to go to my second job as a telephone interviewer[4].

———

Day two. Here we go again. It is another day at an identical McDonald's in some miscellaneous town. This time, I get us there right before

———

4 See "Room with an Interview"

eleven so Kate and I don't have another argument. This one is much slower than the other McDonald's. Thirty minutes go by without a single car. I pour myself samples to kill time as well as to lower our inventory. Since I don't drink soda, I can't tell the difference between this and regular Coke, but definitely don't believe it is good enough to drive mobs of Mid-westerners to McDonald's. It will be like this for much of the day. A few of the employees come outside for a smoke break. I offer—no—demand that they take some samples.

"Quieres una Coke Cero? Tome dos . . . no tres. No me importa. Tengo que usar todo." One guy is leaving for the day and wants a whole can. We had been told that this is not fair game, but that was before we realized they grossly miscalculated the amount of cases needed at each site. I tell the guy he can have the can.

Every five or ten minutes, I look at my watch. This day is moving slower than a license-renewal line at the DMV. I try to steal Kate's cus-tomers—the ones that are clearly walking into the restaurant—by offering them samples before they get in the door. I net a few takers. Every so often, a rolling gold mine comes through the drive-thru, like a giant van packed to the gills with children.

"Hey guys. Free samples. Do you want some? I'm sure your mom won't mind."

I fill a tray with cups and burn through a dozen samples instantly. At 1:50, I start cleaning up. There are still tons of unused sample cups, but it isn't worth it anymore. I take my time rolling the cooler to a corner and dump it. I spend a few minutes putting five more cases into my car and then take the tub inside. Kate is actually on the same page as me this time, and we bolt at 2:15.

"Luego! Gracias!" The workers have a lot of respect for us for some reason. They think we work for Coke and travel all over the country doing this.

———

On day three, we are at a McDonald's close to a high school. At around noon, fifty kids roll in to hang out.

"Hey guys, you want some Coke Zero? The faster I get rid of these, the faster I can leave. Can you help me out?" They swarm like piranhas.

"What's it like working for Coke?"

"Ummmm, pretty awesome. All the free Coke I want."

Many of them offer up their cups for seconds. Others see this and wave me over. This is the closest I have ever been to working as a waiter.

"All right, I'm out. I need to get more Coke. Be right back." I run outside to grab more cans.

"It's madness in there," I tell Kate. "Pure madness."

This day goes by quicker than the other two.

---

It is now day five, and there is a small change. We don't have to drive today because we have been assigned a McDonald's in the city. Hmm, does that say South 63rd? Yes, it does. This McDonald's is located in the heart of Englewood, one of the most dangerous and violent neighborhoods in Chicago. It made national news a couple years earlier for a rash of murders in a short period of time. An honors student was killed by a mob after school, and it was caught on videotape. Foreclosures are on the rise, and people are moving to safer areas where there are jobs.

This could be interesting.

This McDonald's is a block from the end of the Green line, a busy area. It is the hottest day yet, and I choose to be outside in order to soak in the neighborhood scene. It is a Thursday, midday, and there is a buzz of activity already. Immediately, a couple guys come up to me.

"What's going on?" they ask.

"Free Coke Zero. Just a little promotion we are doing." I don't have to tell them twice. They gulp down their cups and ask for seconds. My pleasure. Word gets out fast on the street that Coke Zero is being given out for free. Kids on bikes, families walking by, and the people that were hanging out by the liquor store meander over. It's not even 11:00, and I can't keep up with the demand.

Apparently the same is happening on the inside as well. Kate is constantly back and forth carrying all the cans she can.

I had come into this area with some trepidation, but now I am enjoying myself immensely. People are actually out and about in this neighborhood unlike all of the other McDonald's we have visited. Another guy rolls up on a bike and takes a sample. We chat for a while and I keep filling up his cup, like a bartender topping off a patron's whiskey tumbler.

Time flies by.

The manager comes out and talks to me for a while. He is a fan of the promotion and thinks it has been a big success. This is the first area where I have been by a real sidewalk, so my little setup is attracting dozens of pedestrians. Many of these people aren't even going to McDonald's, but I figure the important thing is that these people know this delicious, zero-calorie beverage can now be found at their local Mickey D's.

People are definitely more aggressive in these parts as well. Some people demand that I give them a whole can, and I acquiesce whenever I can get away with it. But given the high murder rate in the mile radius of where I am standing, things aren't too bad. The day goes by faster than any other, and I arrive home much quicker as well, since I can take a train the whole way.

————————

It is finally the last day of the gig, which makes me happy because it has been a long week. Even though we are only sampling for three hours a day we are out much longer due to travel time. Today, it is just as far away as the one in Indiana, but to the west. This McDonald's is near a town called Batavia and is pretty much halfway to Iowa. As a result, there isn't a whole lot of traffic and the day once again drags. Everything is the same as before with people reacting in the usual way. Most shake their head or politely say no while others get excited about the promotion and choose to take the samples. A few want to know more about the product since it hasn't been in the public eye for a few years. But we were not given a chemical breakdown or the secret recipe. We just know that it has zero calories and that it is supposed to taste like regular Coke. Some people claim to be experts and say Coke Zero tastes like shit or say that they are a Pepsi person.

In the final thirty minutes, a guy comes out of nowhere and asks what we are doing. I give him the usual spiel and offer him a sample. He asks if there is aspartame in the drink, and I say there is.

"You know that stuff kills people right? Causes cancer."

Towards the beginning of the promotion I had actually researched this very claim. After reading several articles, I was convinced that it did *not* cause cancer. As it turns out, aspartame has been around for decades and is one of the most tested sweeteners out there.

"I'm not sure about that," I retort. "I actually just read up on it the other day."

He gets angry and is unconvinced. He can't believe we would have the audacity to sample a product that kills people.

"Sir, I don't make Coke Zero. I'm not a chemist. Don't kill the messenger. Just trying to feed the kids."

He doesn't like this either and huffs off.

And then we are done.

Today, I decide to drive Kate back to her place because I don't have to work my other job. It turns out that she lives in an incredible condo right on Lake Shore Drive overlooking Lake Michigan—prime real estate in Chicago.

After our awkward first day, things had gotten better. She became a little more lenient with the rules. No one ended up coming to check on our progress from the promotion company. I help her unload a few cases of Coke Zero from the trunk, say goodbye, and head home.

———

I think about what I have learned from this gig. I have now seen the kitchen and refrigerators of seven McDonald's all over the Greater Chicago area. I have seen many different drive-thru layouts. I have even seen one McDonald's with a stage that hosts live bands on the weekends. I feel like I wouldn't need an orientation if I got myself a job at one. Plus, I now have 400 cans of Coke Zero to offer my roommates.

Now that I'm done soliciting fast-food patrons, I must refocus my efforts towards soliciting people over the phone at my job downtown.

# ROOM WITH AN INTERVIEW

"Listen. Never call me again, you understand? Better yet. Find a tall building and jump off of it for me."

"All right, sir. Thanks for your time."

Another day, another death threat.

I am on the fifteenth floor of a downtown Chicago high-rise—right at the center of the city, at State and Madison. The most depressing part of my day is when I walk in from the street to conduct phone surveys for the Centers for Disease Control and Prevention (CDC).

"Great atmosphere. Competitive pay. Great experience. Views of Millennium Park. Opportunities for advancement."

It all sounded good in the job advertisement. One month in and I now know that these words are all lies. Looking down at a glaciated valley from a mountaintop is a great atmosphere—a floor full of drones staring at computers and cold calling is decidedly not. Competitive pay seems like it should be more than the minimum wage, but maybe they are comparing our wages to our third world counterparts. Great experience? For what? Sitting in a chair getting yelled at? The views of the park are not bad—that is, if you are at the one computer out of three hundred that is next to the window. I consider myself lucky to have sat there once.

The break room is always buzzing with people blowing off steam during their precious moments away from their computers.

"Man, this lady said these are the kinds of jobs you get when you are dumb. I told her I was just trying to pay for college. I came close to bitchin' her out but kept it cool."

"Some guy told me to get a real job and threatened legal action."

"Another person told me to do something with my life and to fuck off!"

This is normal. Just the other day, a guy kept interrupting me over and over, saying, "WHAT!" each time I started to say something. He finally let me finish before telling me that I was at the bottom of the barrel and to stop being a bottom-feeder.

"Stop fucking calling me!" is a daily occurrence. Threats become so commonplace that, like violence in the media, you become desensitized and numbly move on to the next call.

"Hi, my name is Andrew . . ." Click.

"Hi, my name is Andrew Edwards, calling on behalf of the CDC . . ." Click.

Thirty minutes may go by without ever having someone say more than hello. I have gone entire shifts without completing a single interview. In fact, the company average is about one interview per four-hour shift. This is not an efficient process, but it is one that has been in place since 1994. Apparently, vaccination rates have improved every year since the survey started. I guess that with so many people interviewing around the clock, they do eventually collect enough data to extrapolate.

"We are persistent. We might call people a hundred times if we have to, to see if they are eligible," said my training instructor, and I have seen this first hand.

If another caller has made notes from a previous call, a preview shows up on my screen so that I can see what happened.

"MR sd too busy. gcb."

Male respondent said he was too busy. General callback.

"No AMHH. GCB."

No adult member of the household available. General callback.

I have seen phone numbers that have been called over fifty times. Normally, around the fifth or sixth call, people snap, and that's when the death threats begin. The insider secret to ending the cycle of callbacks (at least until the next quarter) is to say, "Take me off the list." When people hang up without saying anything, it is classified as an invitation to call back in a few days. People don't realize that there is an army of people working from 9:00 a.m. until midnight, dialing constantly. You *will* be called again.

I struggle a bit, wondering if this is a thankless job that is doing good for our society, or a job that shouldn't exist at all. The goal is to get a sample of people from all over the country to see if they are vaccinating their children and are getting them all of the recommended shots. There are other surveys about children with special health care needs. These surveys attempt to find out if parents believe their children are getting the best care possible and how satisfied they are with the health system in general.

The goals of these surveys seem to be admirable, but the methods seem questionable. Paying hundreds of interviewers year-round (even at minimum wage) to complete an interview once every five hours is clumsy and wasteful. This operation costs tens of millions of dollars.

A lot of people answer and immediately announce, "I'm not buying anything or giving any money," and sometimes I want to tell them that as taxpayers, they already have. The company I work for is doing these surveys on behalf of the CDC, which is a government agency, so the millions of dollars they spend annually is a small part of the pot of annual federal taxes. I don't know what the best solution would be: put the money towards campaigns to educate people about vaccinations? Do Internet surveys? Pay participants a nominal fee to complete the surveys?

I think about all of these things because I can as I sit and stare blankly at a grey screen for hours on end. A few weeks ago, I brought reading material. This proved unwise.

"No, no, no. Put that away," says a supervisor who came up stealthily behind me, clearly being as covert as possible.

"Yeah, I understand, but I wasn't getting any cases," I tell him.

"Yes. Yes, you were," he tells me.

*Okaaaaay.*

I put my magazine down and watch as he walks away, smirking. This means I will just have to amuse myself some other way for the remaining hour of my shift. Down the line, five or six people have the same look of anguish, that desperate desire to get out, to be unlocked from their shackles. Then someone will pick up, and they have to talk for a few seconds before the inevitable hang-up, then back to the maddening state of inactivity.

———————

One diversion is listening to all of the ridiculous voice mail messages.

"You've reached Rob. I've got a message for you. Leave a MESSAGE for MEEEEEE!"

"Yo, you know who it is. Holler back."

"This is Kayla. If you want to play games with me, then forget about it. Otherwise, leave me a message and I *might* call you back."

"You know what to do."

"If I know you, leave a message. If not, then hang up and don't ever call me again."

One of the more common ones is this: "Hello? . . . Hello? . . . I'm . . . GOTCHA! I'm not here, but leave a message and I'll hit you back." This one makes you look like an idiot, after responding with hello numerous times, before realizing it is a senseless prank.

Then there are the obligatory family messages, especially around the holidays, where the dad says, "You have," and then the wife says, "reached," and the kids in unison say, "the Hamiltons!" Then altogether they say, "Leave a message!" These make me want to puncture my eardrums with a ballpoint pen.

There are also the ones where a three-year-old kid spends two minutes saying a word every few seconds and you can hear the parents encouraging them to "keep going," and then it finally ends. I begin to mull over the idea of scheduling a vasectomy.

"If you are a telemarketer, you have no place in the world, so hang up now. For everyone else, leave a message."

There are messages where it sounds like there are cars going around a racetrack and you can't understand a word the person is saying. Or people are in bars and you hear dozens of people clinking glasses amidst all sorts of crowd noise. Others have babies crying nonstop in the background. Many people just mumble incoherent nonsense. It's as if people don't know they get more than one shot at recording a message. I can't imagine applying for a job and having a potential employer hear one of these. Ninety percent of the cell phone answering machines don't even mention who it is; it's just a robotic recitation of the ten digits.

———————

Another fun aspect of the job is the fact that all of the interviews are being recorded one hundred percent of the time. Squadrons of supervisors sit in back rooms, listening to everyone's progress. You will be twiddling a pen when one of them pops out of thin air and gives you the "look." It means, sign out to meet with a supervisor and get ready to be told all of the things you were doing wrong.

"So, you were reading the introduction well—I gave you a three for that. Let's talk about this woman a few calls ago. She told you she had no kids, so you kind of skipped forward a couple questions. Yeah . . . yeah, we can't do that. Remember, we have to read the questions verbatim."

"But those questions are talking about kids and I wanted to be more efficient so she wouldn't hang up."

"Yeah, but we have to read the questions verbatim, got it?" This is said while delivering a shit-eating grin.

"Sure," I say.

"Oh, and one more thing. Four weeks ago, we kind of had a problem. You forgot to clock out."

"Whoops. Sorry about that. I don't really remember."

"Yeah, Andrew, it's fine. We just want to give you a friendly reminder now so that it doesn't happen again. Understand?"

"Yeah, got it—no problem."

"All right, Andrew, I think that's it. You can go back to calling people."

"Awesome."

Back to the phones. These meetings are unpleasant, but it is still a good respite from the floor.

———————

There is a suggestion box that I plan on utilizing soon. My first suggestion is for them to lower the temperature in the room. The air is already suffocating enough with the depressive nature of the job and the claustrophobic incarceration of our tiny spaces lined up next to each other row after row. The fact that the thermostat reads seventy-eight degrees adds sweating to the list of discomforts.

Another suggestion would be to revise their recruitment propaganda for this awful position to include a smidgen more truth. Inform people that this job entails sitting in a chair and infuriating people all over the country—people who are trying to do things like read, watch movies, play with their kids, or make unintelligible voicemail messages. And maybe mention that the retirement plan offered isn't available until you have been here a year, which has statistically proven to be impossible. Most people last less than a month here, despite the recession. In the break room, I finally talk to a girl I had seen around.

"How long have you been working here?" I ask.

"Too long." She leaves to go back to the computers.

———————

I have a bad habit of looking at the clock, especially during the last hour of the shift. Time drags almost as slowly as the last few minutes of the night shift at the mail sorting facility. I will go through an entire four-hour shift without an interview and then at the three hour and fifty-nine minute mark, I press the "hand" on the screen, which means this will be my final call. All right, a quick hang-up or an answering machine, and I am out of here.

However, the gods are not that generous. Suddenly, the nicest person in the world picks up. I mumble softly to see if they will hang up. Nope. They are all about the survey and will answer all of the questions no matter how long it takes. They believe the CDC is doing a great job and they will go the extra mile with this survey. I end up rolling out at 8:20.

People say that if you love your job, it doesn't feel like work at all. I have succeeded in finding the contrapositive of this scenario, or perhaps something in the middle. I have discovered a job I absolutely hate but it doesn't exactly feel like work either. Every time I walk in here, it feels like I am entering an episode of *The Twilight Zone* and that something just isn't right. All I know is that I have to get out as soon as possible.

# IT'S SOY NICE TO MILK YOU

"Free vanilla almond milk samples! Try some Silk—the alternative to milk!"

I am on Michigan Avenue in Chicago, near the river, wearing a jetpack full of almond milk. The bladder containing the liquid is cleverly concealed within a large milk carton replica. As pedestrians walk by, I offer samples, dispensing them by squirting milk into a small cup.

A week earlier, I had responded to a Craigslist ad for a street marketing campaign and received a call back the next day.

"So Andrew, we have a great promotion here—going to be a lot of fun! You're going to wear a huge jetpack full of Silk milk products and walk all over Chicago getting people excited about our brand!"

"Cool," I responded, masking my disdain.

"Just get the paperwork back to me, and we'll be set."

After receiving a degree in accounting, this was not the type of job I thought I'd be working at age twenty-eight. It takes a certain kind of person to get decked out in a Silk visor and a Silk jacket, asking strangers to try some soymilk from a giant Silk carton strapped to your back. I am not that kind of person. I wear baseball caps, not visors.

---

It is the first day of the gig. There is a huge tent serving as our home base near the Tribune Tower with all sorts of stuff, including cereal, so people can see how soymilk and almond milk stack up against the traditional kind. After getting filled up with product we head to the sidewalk.

"Get your soymilk samples here," I all but whisper to dozens of people as they shuffle by, engrossed in their cell phones.

"Soymilk sample, sir?" I mumble incoherently again.

Five minutes down—nine hours and fifty-five minutes to go.

An hour in, I am standing next to two other dudes: one guy is Chocolate Soymilk and the other is Dark Chocolate Almond Milk.

"This is the worst-run promotion I have ever worked," exclaims Dark Chocolate Almond Milk.

There are people who make a living doing promotions year-round; these guys are two of them. Promotion lifers give away samples of everything while wearing just about any variety of outlandish outfits you can think of. They aggressively push people to sign up for reward accounts. They maintain 1,000-watt smiles and unabashedly force themselves on strangers without any hesitation. I am slowly becoming a promotion veteran myself, but have no aspirations of upgrading to a year-round ambassador. I would be happy never exuding false enthusiasm for money again.

These two guys have worked dozens of similar gigs, so I ask them what is so bad about this one. They say Mitchell, the guy heading the promotion, is worthless and mean. I agree with this, but really don't care either way. He is probably the unhappiest, angriest looking character I have ever seen, which at first is disconcerting, but later becomes entertaining. He glares at us all day, seemingly waiting for us to fuck up so that he can scream at us. He is able to keep up this demeanor all week without ever cracking a smile. If I delegated work to a bunch of temps and didn't do shit, I would be smiling constantly. I am walking around giving out samples of almond milk on a Friday afternoon—you can't take things like this too seriously.

However, Dark Chocolate can't seem to get over his beef with Mitchell.

"Those girls shouldn't have to carry around these jetpacks for so long. This is fucking bullshit. All right, I'm going on my break." He walks away.

Five minutes later, Chocolate Soymilk comes by and asks me if I saw what went down. I did not.

"The Almond Milk guy went ape-shit on Mitchell and got himself fired!"

Apparently he used his break to let Mitchell know exactly how the operation should be run, and was promptly fired—two hours into a week-long job. Impressive.

---

The structure of these things is always interesting. Mitchell and the other two managers awkwardly walk around doing absolutely nothing. These guys have been doing this for months, since it's a nationwide product promotion. Really, their only job is to refill our jetpacks. I am extremely generous in sampling so that my pack depletes as quickly as possible in order to keep the weight manageable.

"Done," I tell Tanya, one of the leads.

"Okay. Why don't you help sample here under the tent, and we'll reload ya."

It ends up being a long day, but the time does go by fairly quickly because of the stream of sample patrons. The rest of the days will be different. We will be on the move and will go all over the downtown area.

"Hey guys," Krystal with a K says. "Millennium Park. Tomorrow at 11:00." I nod and head home.

My back is sore, but not too bad. The longest day is over. The remaining six days will only be five-hour shifts, or so says the schedule.

---

I arrive at 10:55 a.m. the next morning. At 11:05, everyone (minus the dude Mitchell canned yesterday) is here. Everyone except the supervisors.

It is now 11:15. One of the guys gets a text from "management."

"Guys, running a little late. Go hang out in the park."

What the fuck? We grumble amongst ourselves. What does "a little late" mean? Why are they late when all they have to do is drive downtown in the Silkmobile? I had to take a series of buses and trains. One dude came here all the way from the burbs.

11:30. Nothing.

11:45. Still chillin'.

Noon. *Okaaaaay.*

12:15. We finally get another text.

"All right, guys. We're in an alley across the street." We walk over, and I assume we will receive an immediate apology for wasting over an hour of our lives.

Nope.

"Guys. Let's start making bags." We form small assembly lines and throw coupons into reusable canvas bags—coupons and bags I will later see in the gutters and garbage cans. We continue for thirty minutes and then wait even longer while the supervisors fill our jetpacks.

I just waited an hour for a bunch of idiots. Now, I am standing in a dark and filthy alley, assembling cheap swag, waiting to put on a thirty-five-pound jetpack full of soymilk. I start to question where things had gone wrong in my life. I would have lost it then, had I not discovered another real person in our group—a filmmaker named Mike[5]. Like me, he does not do gigs like this often and sort of stumbled upon it. For the rest of the promotion, we will celebrate the absurdity of the gig together and take it as un-seriously as we can manage.

We come up with ridiculous hooks to try to get people to take a sample. Someone comes up with, "Once you go Silk, you never go milk."

We were supposed to memorize all of the nutritional information of the five varieties we are sampling, but I never bothered. If people ask, I either make something up or tell them to check out the milk carton in the store.

---

5 Mike Brune is the talented filmmaker who directed and edited my Kickstarter video for this book.

The biggest mystery of the promotion is the feverish interest generated by the reusable bags. These are cheap, shitty, small blue bags that say Silk on them. If someone offered me one, I would walk the other way. I guess I am not the target demographic for shitty blue bags.

As soon as we start to assemble the bags, even in a sketchy alley, people flock to us like vultures on roadkill.

"Can I get one for my husband?"

"Sure. Take fifty."

People seem to think these bags are the greatest things since sliced bread. Some people approach us already carrying ten bags from shopping and other things.

"Need another bag?" I ask sarcastically, and ninety-five percent of the time the response is yes.

We have some people handing out bags and others putting them together. Passersby make off with them as soon as they are put out. Taxis will cross multiple lanes of traffic to try to get a free bag. A security guard inside one of the buildings sees us outside and when I go in for a drink, he asks me for a free bag.

What I think is the dumbest freebee ever turns out to be a blockbuster hit.

After we get rid of the bags, the supervisors order us to walk to various areas so they can take marketing pictures of us. I pray that I will not be seen by anyone I know. They line us up in front of statues, in front of the *Bean*, in front of the Water Tower, all over. Then they take pictures while hundreds of tourists look on in bewilderment. After all, you don't see squadrons of jetpack-wielding samplers every day.

We are not afforded explanations for why we are doing this or where these pictures are going. For my sake, I hope they disappear. Some people go nuts when they see us. They take pictures with us and want to wear the jetpacks around. I politely smile, simultaneously pondering the meaning of life.

———

It is day five of the promotion. I purposely show up fifteen minutes late because I don't care any more.

There is a new tactic today. I pause to look closer because I don't believe it. Instead of putting coupons in the bags, we are putting half-gallon milk containers into them. We are on a side street right in the heart of downtown during morning rush hour. Once again, we cannot hand these things out fast enough. We are passing out hundreds and hundreds of bags with Silk milk in them. The best part is the look on people's faces when they accept the bag from us expecting it to be empty, only to find it heavy because it has an entire milk carton inside. I can't help but wonder where people are going to put the milk. It has to be refrigerated, but since every-one is going to work, how is that supposed to happen?

My thoughts are interrupted when Mitchell screams, "We need more milk! Faster!"

We are told to tell people that it needs to be refrigerated, but I can't imagine more than five percent actually hearing us, or giving a shit. I still wonder what happened to all of the people who drank unrefrigerated soy-milk that day. Oh well. Not my problem. Just following orders.

After the great rush hour milk giveaway, it is back to the jetpacks and touring downtown. In these parts we get more business types and fewer tourists, and as a result, fewer takers.

One guy in a suit grumbles as he walks by, "I bet your parents would be proud."

Most people are indifferent, with the exception of the numerous panhandlers, who are all very fond of the free samples.

"One more, for the road," says one woman who is on sample num-ber fifteen.

———

Even as the promotion wraps up, I never learn much about the rest of our crew.

One guy is an on-and-off English teacher abroad. One girl is from Mississippi, studying nursing in Chicago. Another graduated from Columbia College over a year earlier. I don't know about the rest. Besides Mike the filmmaker, and me, the others are all veterans of the promotional scene.

The English teacher stares blankly, sticks his arm outward with a sample, and says, "Soymilk. Get a sample. It's good," without a trace of emotion and doesn't care one bit if he is denied. I am the exact opposite and feel like I am being a burden by annoying people with unwanted milk-pushing.

---

As we finish the last day, we grab several cartons to take home with us and inquire about whether we will have to work the next day. Originally, they had said that some of the group would work an eighth day, at a 5K run downtown. They say they'll let us know.

Mike and I look at each other.

Okay, it's Friday night and tomorrow's shift starts at 6:00 a.m. When are they going to let us know? Why doesn't anybody ever know anything? Are we supposed to wait around all night waiting for a call? I know we are wearing jetpacks, but this isn't rocket science. In the end, neither of us receives a call, which is ideal.

On the bright side, I was able to try a bunch of alternative milks and might even convert to the soy and almond world. Just don't ask me about the health benefits.

# GROUPON AND OFF AGAIN

I am at a local discount clothing store looking for a cheap pair of jeans. I haven't worn jeans since elementary school and need a pair for a one-day gig happening a week from now.

The job is for Groupon, a quickly expanding local deals operator. We will be promoting the launch of their new service called Groupon Now, in which businesses offer deals for a limited time on a given day. For example, if a company knows that Mondays are usually slow, they may do a Groupon Now deal offering twenty dollars of food for fifteen dollars. If patrons happen to be in the area and are looking for something to do, they enter the zip code on the Groupon website or smart phone application, and all of the deals within a certain radius will pop up.

Right now, all I know is that I need to get a pair of jeans and show up at Millennium Park on Friday. The hiring process was a thirty-second phone call followed by an email with the necessary paperwork attached. Apparently, this will be a promotion of epic proportions that will take the city by storm, and they are hiring as many people as they can get. They had offered five-dollar referral fees to anyone who could find other people to join the promotion. I emailed the guy the contact information for my friend Jessica. She had the job a day later.

———————

It is Friday. Jessica and I meet at 6:45 a.m. The organizers insisted that everyone arrive extremely early because it is such an important promotion.

We foolishly get to Millennium Park a couple minutes before seven, sign in, and then are asked to sit down and wait . . . for twenty minutes.

Well over a hundred people have ambled over to sign in and eventually we hear murmurings about heading over to the *Bean*. Nobody knows who is in charge, so we just start walking. We approach a scene of pure chaos. Even more people have come out of the woodwork. There is a woman screeching on a megaphone as she tries, and fails, to dispatch a rowdy group of brand ambassadors. Jessica and I continue to trudge behind other people, like attendees at a state fair.

Someone yells out that she needs twelve people, so a few of us gravitate towards her. She counts twelve, but two friends have been separated, so she needs to recount. Someone else leaves the group, so she tries to get another person to join. Five minutes and several more miscounts later, our group is formed. We are a ragtag squad that will be a team for this promotion. In all, there will be fifteen groups canvassing the city, trying to cover as many of Chicago's neighborhoods as possible.

We are handed our gear for the day: a cross-body messenger bag with freebies and our Groupon shirt inside. The shirt is a bright pea green that absolutely no one looks good in. It is truly hideous. Our bags contain oversized sunglasses, fake bling, cowbells, fake tattoos, and an assortment of other useless items that will be our tools to attract attention.

After thirty minutes, all of the groups have formed and we find out what we'll do for the promotion. We are to tell people that all of the Groupon Now deals will be one dollar today. One dollar for a meal, one dollar for a spa treatment, one dollar for anything. The catch is that you need to have a computer close by, or more realistically, a smart phone. Before hitting the streets, we take our mandatory group photo on the steps in front of the *Bean*. Our outfits are strictly enforced. Blue jeans, tennis shoes, and no hat. The photographer gets the group riled up, and we all let loose a scream of excitement for the picture. It is a pathetic sight. Over a hundred adults without real jobs about to promote products we can't afford on smart phones we don't own.

---

Now it's go time. Everyone receives CTA transit passes to get to their destinations, but our group has been assigned the Water Tower area of Michigan Avenue, which is only a mile away. I suggest walking rather than taking the train, and say that we should do a mobile promotion while we commute to our designated location.

For better or worse, it turns out that Jessica and I have the rowdiest group imaginable. As soon as we start down the street, two of the guys start screaming without any inhibition about Groupon Now. They have either done a lot of promotions or simply don't give a shit about yelling at complete strangers. Other than handing out a few cards with instructions on accessing the deals, we are supposed to be a presence and get the word out.

Not only do we have a raucous crew, but our group leader, Kim, is very laid back and doesn't care what we do. We walk by high-end jewelry and clothing stores and aggressively get in people's faces, asking them if they are aware of the "crazy" deals going on all day. Since there are no Groupon authorities on our team, we have just embarked on an all day extravaganza of walking around screaming things that we come up with. A few of us have huge signs that make us look like protesters. We wave and twirl them around, drawing as much attention as possible.

We finally get to our assigned area and break up to cover different corners. Jessica and I go off on our own to hang by the Old Water Tower, one of the few buildings to survive the Great Chicago Fire of 1871. It is Jessica's first-ever promotional gig, and she isn't sure how to go about it. Her naturally gregarious personality makes it easy. I tell her we just need to talk to people. As usual, many people are in a hurry, or think we are selling something, so they look down and avoid us like we are lepers. Still, many people do show interest.

Our main pitch is: Dollar deals! Every deal is a dollar! Boat rides. Haircuts. Lunch. Dinner. One. Dollar. No joke. This is for real!

One of the first people to respond is all over it. It is a guy who has taken the day off in order to take full advantage of the deal. So far, he has spent twelve dollars for twelve deals, with the intention of taking a river architectural tour, visiting the Hancock Tower viewing platform, going out for lunch, taking Tae Kwan Do lessons, getting ice cream, in addition to several other activities. He is having problems purchasing another deal and inquires about quotas or limits on deals. We tell him that we know nothing. He knows much more than we do, so all we can do is wish him luck.

Kim comes out of nowhere looking for two of the girls in our group. We tell her that we haven't seen anyone. It seems they have gone off on their own somewhere, either hitting a different part of town or hanging out on Groupon's dime.

She says, "Oh well," and tells us we can hit our lunch break.

We go to the cafeteria in the Water Tower mall. I get my food, and Jessica comes over a couple minutes later.

"I just paid fifteen dollars for this salad. I just spent an hour yelling shit about Groupon for five pieces of lettuce." Her salad is miniscule and obviously a complete rip-off.

"Yeesh," I say. Still, it is good to be out of the sun. As an avid hat wearer, the no-hat rule has not been kind to me. It is ninety degrees and very bright. I will spend the rest of the day using the sign as an umbrella and seeking shade whenever possible.

———————

An hour later, everyone has taken a break, and Kim tells us that we are mobilizing. We have a situation at a steakhouse about a mile away. The dollar deal is for a rib lunch that retails for twenty-five dollars. A long line has formed, and they need entertainment.

We reconvene and people get out their cowbells and whistles and start marching.

"Dollar deals! You can't even ride the CTA for a dollar!"

"Okay, deals . . . where are they? RIGHT HERE! ALL DAY! ONE DOLLAR! HIT. IT. UP."

We get increasingly more rowdy and feel that we can do anything. I am actually into it now because I am not wearing a giant milk carton or giving away worthless crap. I just need to get the word out about some great deals. Without supervision or a set protocol, the scene is perfect for outlandish improvisation. On the way to the steakhouse, we try to outdo each other with ridiculous chants and pitches.

"You want to eat dinner for a dollar tonight? Impossible? POSSI-BLE. Get out your smart phone, and we'll show you how." Jessica and I don't have smart phones, so we stand idle when people actually do inquire about how it works. A few people in the group show inquisitive pedestrians how it is done.

"One dollar for a Qdoba burrito. Right now. Oh, one dollar for drinks at that bar you are looking at. No big deal. Actually, it's a sick deal. Go do it!"

We arrive at the restaurant where about fifty people are waiting outside. We have been told to entertain them. Apparently, Jessica and I are the only ones that feel this is an awkward proposition and hang back. But as usual, our crew gets the job done. One of them immediately starts a chant.

"I say GROUPON! You say NOW! GROUPON! NOW! GROU-PON! NOW! I say DOLLAR! You say DEALS! DOLLAR! DEALS! DOLLAR! DEALS!"

The crowd is into it. Someone inflates a Groupon beach ball and starts batting it up and down the line. People take our Groupon sunglasses like we are giving away Benjamins. I decide to talk to the people at the front of the line. They have been here for over forty-five minutes and are getting frustrated. The restaurant did not prepare for this, and it has become a disastrous situation. A worker dripping with sweat, clearly hating his life, comes out and yells for Thomas, Cyndi, and Arthur. Their lunches are ready. Kim tells a few of us to hang out at another block, so I find one with some shade. About twenty minutes later, the guys from the front of the rib line walk by me without anything in their hands. They are sick of waiting and don't want to get in trouble at work.

---

A little while later, we head back towards Michigan Avenue. Jessica and I stay out of the way and innocently raise our Groupon signs. In contrast, the rest of our squad heads straight into restaurant patios, parking lots, streets, and alleys, addressing anyone and everyone with feverish energy. They are pulling the load for us big time. Although the servers don't seem to enjoy mobs of promoters harassing their seated patrons, people are definitely interested in what we are pushing. We set up camp at a busy intersection on Michigan Avenue. With our pea green shirts and wacky accessories, we have succeeded in garnering a lot of attention for Groupon. Kids want to take pictures with us, and people come up to inquire what the deal is, no Groupun intended.

It is now 4:00 p.m., and we have two hours left. Kim says she thinks we have done a great job and since we don't have any more fliers to hand out, we can leave after another twenty minutes.

Our group heads back to the Water Tower, still trying to one-up each other's pitches. When a person is getting a cab, we tell her that it will cost her three dollars just to sit down, and for three dollars she could take tango lessons, eat some ice cream, and get drinks at the Public House. We are going overboard, invading personal bubbles, but we are having fun.

A businessman walks by. "A nine percent return on your Fidelity portfolio is too good to be true. Dollar deals all day is *not* too good to be true. I will show you twenty deals within four blocks from here. Come on over."

"You think any size drink for one dollar at McDonalds is a deal? A two-hour dinner cruise on Lake Michigan for a dollar is a deal."

Before long, we are told to wrap it up and go home. I am eager to donate my shirt and bag to the same store where I picked up my jeans. Jessica and I backtrack to her apartment to look for Groupon Now deals on her computer. We go to a place on Rush Street for dinner and get dollar ice creams afterwards to celebrate a job well done.

# FREE TENTERTAINMENT

I enter a huge ballroom at the downtown Chicago Marriott. There are about a hundred young people sitting in chairs that line the edge of the room. I arrive just in time for the training session for a flash mob event being sponsored by Coleman, but being run by a company called Garbage Media. We wait in a freezing room for twenty minutes until the organizer, Mike, finally arrives to address us.

"Okay, guys. Let's sign in up here at the table. After you do that, grab a tent."

All one hundred people descend upon the table like shoppers at a Black Friday Walmart sale. I remain seated for another fifteen minutes until the line dwindles to five people. After I sign my name on a paper, I am told to pair up with Felix, the guy behind me, and practice opening and closing the tent we are promoting.

We open up the package, pull out the bulky tent, and try to figure out how to set it up. The special thing about this tent is that it has all of its poles attached and can be assembled in less than a minute. As promised by the blurb on the package, our tent is pitched in a flash. We see others struggle, attempting to erect the tent over and over to no avail. We are content with our one successful effort and are ready to get the show on the road. We have now been here for forty-five minutes and have done nothing but open up a tent.

After a while, Mike tells us to sit so that we can watch our training video—except the projector doesn't work. They have to call someone from downstairs to come and mess with it. I close my eyes and try to relax.

Eventually they get it to work, and the video begins. The actors tell us we will be part of a super-exciting campaign for Coleman Tents, promoting their new pop-up tent, which is the easiest tent ever made. We are going to take Chicago by storm and show them what Coleman is all about. Then we get to the meat of the program—the flash dance.

The guy and girl in the video each hold part of the tent and start marching up and down like soldiers, chanting, "C-O-L-E-M-A-N! COLE-MAN! COLEMAN! COLEMAN!"

I look for the nearest exit.

*You've got to be kidding me.*

They walk around each other, then one of them opens up the tent bag, and they quickly assemble the tent. When they are done, they get down on their knees in front of the tent, their faces beaming with identical smiles of pure joy.

"And that's it. We will have over one hundred people putting up fifty tents in under a minute. It's going to be an amazing event."

People are not impressed, but it is what it is and we get up to practice. I stay with Felix, and we go out in the hallway to prepare our entrance. We walk in and line up in several rows like a marching band during the halftime of a football game. The leader blows a whistle, and it is go time. We unzip the package and set up the tent in under a minute. We then crawl into it and scream wildly to let everyone know how fun these tents are and how easy they are to set up.

We hear another whistle, and we have to undo everything. Felix and I have it down, but several other groups can't fit the tents back in their bags. We have to practice the routine another ten times to make sure everyone can do it perfectly. Finally, after two hours of training for something that should have taken ten minutes, we are dismissed and told to meet downtown the next day for the live performance at 10:00 a.m.

I am the first one out the door.

------

The next day, I arrive just in time again. This is a mistake. The leaders of the operation are running around like chickens with their heads cut off and are nowhere near ready to organize us. A hundred of us are doing the flash mob, and another fifteen or so have been placed right on Michigan Avenue to run the fake campground, where a few tents are set up next to all sorts of camping gear. Their job is to explain the promotion to passersby and to drive pedestrian traffic towards our performances. Their position is much worse than ours; they have to stand the entire time and interact with people about a shitty product. The promotion leaders are dealing with them right now and tell us to hold tight. We mill around and talk amongst ourselves.

Eventually, Mike returns. He divides us into groups and distributes green Coleman T-shirts that will serve as our uniform for the day. We then move in close together and get our pep talk.

"All right, guys. This is it. Get excited. Remember, one whistle is the cue to unzip. Second whistle, we roll. I want you guys to be loud. Let's do it!"

We line up, and fortunately Felix and I are assigned to one of the back rows.

It's time. We start marching.

There is a girl in front who has been put in charge of the chant. She counts us off.

"ONE! TWO! THREE! FOUR!"

We start chanting, "C-O-L-E-M-A-N!"

As we chant, we throw our fists in the air like soldiers heading to war. We start between two buildings and make our way down a side street towards Michigan Avenue. We keep up the ruckus all the way to Pioneer Square. Confused tourists look on in amazement while others maintain their distance. Just like with the soymilk gig, I pray that I don't see anyone I know.

I continue to chant and pump my fists as we make the last turn and file into our designated rows. I look out onto the sidewalk and see approximately seven non-Coleman people who have stopped to see what is going on.

One whistle.

Felix unzips the tent bag.

Wait for it . . . there's the second whistle.

We spring into action and dominate as always.

We jump inside the tents, and all one hundred of us scream like madmen. We shake our tents and some people start a "Coleman! Coleman!" cheer, while others abandon words entirely and go nuts.

Then another whistle.

We jump out of our tent and stand next to it.

Now the last whistle.

We break it down, stuff it in the bag, and sit by the bag with one knee on the ground, showing the observers how easy it is. The same girl counts us off and we cheer again as we make our exit.

We go back to the fountain area where we had gathered in the morning. The performance lasted approximately five minutes. Now what do we do?

Several people have to go to the bathroom and ask Mike about taking a break. Because some people had gone before our first performance and caused a substantial disturbance, he says we can go but it will be the last break we have.

This nearly causes a riot amongst our ranks. We still have four hours left to go.

Felix puts down his forty-eight ounce drink container.

"Maybe . . . I'll save this for later."

People start griping, but I decide we should probably go while we can. I know of a nice bathroom in the basement of an office building nearby and lead a group of people there. Mike intercepts us as we make our way down the escalator.

"You guys can't use this bathroom. You'll have to find another one."

*Okay, hard-ass.*

We tell him it's cool, and mill around until he takes off. I tell the group to stick with me and to take the Coleman shirts off so that we'll be less conspicuous. I find a pedway that wraps around to another part of the building. No bathrooms here.

Screw it. I decide to take us back to the ones I know. We peek around the corner, see that Mike isn't there, and scramble along the wall to get to the bathrooms. After we are done, I ask if anyone is hungry. We go to an upscale food court and order food but aren't sure if we should bring our meals back to the main Coleman group or eat them here. We decide to stay put so that Mike won't see us with food and get pissed. I order soup, which is difficult to eat quickly, but I do the best I can, and we take a back way out to the fountain.

Uh-oh.

Everyone is huddled around listening to Mike. We creep in as quietly and as stealthily as possible. He is saying something about taking advantage of breaks. Next time, if people aren't back in five minutes, they won't be getting paid. Point taken. Still, it was a nice thirty-minute break.

We hang out for another few minutes until it is time for round two. We get in formation once again, and the crazy girl in front starts us off. This time there are maybe twelve people watching. I try to calculate how much money Coleman is wasting today. Let's see: fifty crappy tents, hotel ballroom rental for excessive flash dance practice, and wages for one hundred under-employed, chanting dopes, and a team of grouchy, unprepared supervisors. Whatever the amount is, it's a shitload.

The performance goes off without a hitch and we retreat to home base. A lot of people lie down next to the fountain and use the tents as pillows. Others hang out and talk. I learn that Felix is originally from Guatemala and lives in Northern Indiana. He was running late this morning so he took a cab from the train station to get here on time. He was not pleased that he had to wait for thirty minutes before anything happened. Like many of these people, Felix is a promotional guy who does all sorts of things like this. He has two other regular gigs—one working a photo booth at events like weddings and parties, and another promoting Vitamin Water at events around the area. Several other people talk about an alcohol promotion they have recently done. Many are students, and I would guess that the average age is about twenty-three.

All right, our break is over. Time for round three.

It does not get less embarrassing with repetition, but we grind through it.

The two people next to us have broken their tent. One of the poles won't go up or down, so their tent looks like a bear mauled it. Over the course of the five performances, many of the tents will break in some manner. These tents are not high quality. Coleman is known for budget tents, and these don't disappoint. There is a reason they are only sold at Kmarts and Walmarts, and not real outdoor equipment stores. They weigh about ten pounds, take up a ton of space, and they're only a viable option for car camping. Several of us notice that there is no rainfly, but we don't inquire about it. We are paid to make fools of ourselves, but we don't have to explain the tent specs to inquiring minds. That is the job of the ambassadors at the fake tent site in front of us. After we finish another round of our tent dance, they must continue to field questions and stand around awkwardly.

We return to the fountain and lie down to catch some rays. We are now sixty percent of the way done, and there is light at the end of the tunnel. It is beautiful out and I just want to get out of here.

————————

Ten minutes of actual work and ninety minutes of lounging and we are done. We gather around Mike who says we did a great job and that we get to keep the T-shirts!

We line up to sign out so we can get paid. This time, I don't wait for everyone else and get in line quickly so I can get the hell out of here.

# IN A STUPOR WALMART

I apply to be a part of a team of eight promotional models working a one-day gig in suburban Chicago. We will let people know that the Walmart is now a Super Walmart, complete with food and other great things at incredible prices. I get called back the same day from the marketing company running the promotion.

"So Andrew, are you able to show up in two days for this thing?"

"Sure."

"You're hired."

───────────

When I arrive two days later, I discover that as always, the team is ragtag. There is an eighteen-year-old woman from Streamwood who says she is a model.

*Hmmmm.*

Maybe I would believe this if there were a hundred people left in the world. She has her hair in an unkempt bun and is wearing way too much makeup for this kind of gig. I imagine her having a boyfriend that wears wife beaters in order to show off his tattoos.

Another girl shows up forty-five minutes late because of train trouble only to find out that she isn't needed. One guy has no undershirt and has the top two buttons of his shirt undone, an apparent homage to Burt Reynolds. A different girl brags about how she has done *so* many promotional gigs all over. Then there is a mother and daughter combo. The mom barely speaks any English so she spends a lot of time idling and staying out of the way.

The dress code for the day: black pants, black shoes, and a long-sleeved, white-collared shirt, tucked in.

The forecast for today: ninety-five degrees and ninety percent humidity. I have a few minutes to spare so I buy some sunscreen, one of the many super products one can get at this place.

The supervisor asks if we have any preference for positions to start off the day. "Inside greeter, giving away freebies?" My hand shoots up immediately. "All right, Andrew, you can go inside now if you'd like."

In ten seconds, I go from ninety-five degrees to air-conditioning in my face; a veteran move. I end up standing next to a Walmart greeter named Sevitana. I ask her where she is from and she makes me guess. I say Bosnia, and she is stunned that I am right. She says people normally guess Russia, Poland, Mexico, and lots of other countries that aren't even close, but never Bosnia. I talk to her and hand out Walmart jar openers and Walmart paper pads. Every single person takes them, many ask for more.

A few minutes later, I get moved to the other door so that we aren't discriminating between entrances. Now I am next to a sixty-year-old woman who is working her third day as a greeter and she loves her job.

"The Target down the street—they were only offering eight hours a week. Walmart is where it's at."

"Definitely," I say. "This is a super-chill place to hang. That's why I came out here, too."

A woman approaches and announces that her daughter is missing. She is half-worried and half-infuriated. She has one kid in tow, but the other one disappeared a while ago. The managers get out their walkie-talkies and start searching. After a few minutes, one of them brings the kid.

"You're gonna get a beating when we get home!" she screams at the child.

I start to get barraged with questions about where the watermelons or Slip 'N Slides are located.

"No idea. I don't work here. Sorry."

Then the ride comes to an end.

The eighteen-year-old "model" comes in and says, "Cotton candy."

"Super," I reply.

Little do I know, but the next seventy-five minutes will be some of the most miserable of my life.

I walk out the door and a blast of hot, humid air slams into my face. There are dozens of kids milling around grabbing free popcorn and cotton candy. The parking lot, which has a larger surface area of concrete than JFK airport, is full. One of the workers comes over to train me on the cotton candy machine for thirty seconds, and then I am on my own. For the next hour, I don't look up once. An infinite line of kids and parents eagerly wait for their helpings.

I grab a paper cone, stick my hand into the machine, and rotate it around inside so the spun sugar accumulates. I more or less get the hang of it but realize after two seconds that my shirt is ruined. Hot air from the machine is blowing in my face and getting sticky, sugary stuff on my shirt, on my glasses, and all over.

And the kids just keep coming.

"I want a red one."

*You're getting a blue one and you're going to like it, you brat.*

"Well, right now we are doing blue. Sorry guys."

The gloves given to us are the worst gloves ever made. They keep getting stuck in the machine, and I nearly get my finger jammed in the motor. No time to worry about that. More kids have arrived.

"Andrew, you ready for your break?" asks the supervisor.

*Thank God.*

I take off my gloves and turn around.

"Wait, wait, I'm looking at this wrong. You're not going for another half an hour."

*Noooooooo!*

I am super pissed. I don't know if I can handle thirty more minutes of sweating my ass off in ninety-five-degree weather being sprayed with gooey sugar, but I manage somehow.

Finally, another girl comes over to relieve me, but I have to train her. This eats into six precious seconds of my break. I quickly walk to the bathroom to wash the powdery sugar off of my hands and arms. I will have to clean my glasses later because I don't have a pressure washer with me at the moment.

I need to get away from the Walmart area and decide to go to a nearby strip mall taquería. As I walk over, I wonder if I should just throw my shirt away after the gig or salvage it at the dry cleaner. I also wonder why we were asked to wear nice clothes to work at a carnival.

---

The thirty minutes go by in a flash. I return and notice that there are no supervisors anywhere, so I designate myself the position furthest from the cotton candy machine—the test-your-strength game and the bags game. I can't think of a more dangerous game for children to play than the strength game. Parents encourage their five-year-olds to whack it as hard as they can. The mallet is half as big as these children. Oftentimes, the kids will miss and hit their feet instead. Other times, another kid will walk by when another is back-swinging, and we have to pull them away before they get nailed in the face. The worst part is the bell. When someone hits it hard enough, which ends up being about ninety percent of the time, the bell goes off, making me cringe because of how loud it is. For the kids, it's so much fun! Some of the bigger kids like to slam it over and over until they are dragged away by their parents.

I retire the mallet and begin to promote baggo, or cornhole. In this game, players try to toss beanbags into holes cut out of boxes. It is conveniently set up right next to where cars are zooming by in the parking lot, so if a kid misfires on a throw, the bag ends up in traffic. Not a good idea, guys.

Soon, we run out of cotton candy and popcorn, which nearly causes a riot. People swarm to the table, and demand to know where the free cotton candy is.

"Sorry, it's gone."

People give us looks of disgust and walk away.

Now, we really have to push the baggo game. It's all we have, except for the lucky ducky game, which isn't going so well. People have realized they will get a piece of candy no matter which duck they pick, so there is no element of surprise.

The plant-a-seed-in-a-cup is also a bust because we ran out of soil in the first hour. Kids aren't too interested in coloring their own picture frames at the adjacent booth, either. Cotton candy and smashing things with a hammer was our gold mine, but we have shut them down. To stem the tide, I allow a four-year-old Indian girl to try the strength game. She fails in her three attempts. Just then, a modern day Dennis the Menace comes on the scene. Apparently his mom is inside shopping and left him out here to wreak havoc.

He grabs the mallet from the girl and says, "Watch me do it," and smashes it five times in a row. He is three times bigger than her and is way too big to be playing.

I finally snap. "All right, I think we've had enough of the test-your-strength game for a while. Go get more candy."

When he returns, I challenge him to a baggo duel and destroy him over and over. He still has cotton candy all over his face and is jumping around like a madman.

"Where is your mom again?" I ask him. After an eternity, a woman emerges from the store, lights up a cigarette, and yells at the kid to get in the car. Finally.

Then the white trash crew arrives. Is it my coworker's boyfriend? They think this is a real carnival and hang out even though there is no longer anything going on and all of the games are for five-year-olds. They gather around to watch the mom half of the mother-daughter combo challenge people at baggo. We have a PA system, and the model does a play-by-play. More people gather; there is now a crowd watching with rapt attention as the mom demolishes the competition. I pace back-and-forth in the background, looking at my watch every couple of minutes, hoping time speeds up.

At four o'clock, the supervisor who hasn't been around the entire day announces that we can start breaking down. I jump up and start throwing things in boxes. The supervisor announces that they are doing this gig again in two weeks at the Walmart in Antioch, which is fifty miles north of Chicago.

*Yeah . . . not sure about that one.*

She tosses me her car keys and tells us to put stuff in the trunk.

*Yes, your highness.*

I smash things into her car and ask if anything else needs to be done. Nope. Looks like that's it. I buy some glass cleaner solution and drive away, hoping to never see this Walmart again.

# CARI . . . BOU CARES?

I arrive at a park near Lake Michigan where I play in an ultimate summer league. I receive a call regarding a promotion I am starting tomorrow at the Taste of Chicago.

"Hi Andrew, this is Fatma, the lead on the Caribou Coffee promotion. Small change in plans. Can I give you all of the shirts and materials for tomorrow? I'm not sure I can get there early enough in the morning since I am working on this other thing."

I am a little confused by this, and then tell her that I'm at an ultimate game and won't be done until eight, and after that, I will go to an improv show and won't get home until midnight. I tell her that I have roommates and that she can probably dump the stuff off with them.

Apparently that works for her, because when I get home there are a few boxes sitting on the ground containing several Caribou Coffee shirts and thousands of coffee reward cards. Suddenly, I'm in charge of this gig? I read an email from Fatma explaining how everything will go down. I have read short novels with fewer words.

"We will be convening at Michigan and Jackson. Sue will arrive fifteen minutes prior to activation and then . . . " Blah. Blah. Blah. The only thing that I get from this is that we will be giving out Caribou Coffee reward cards to people. That's it.

———————

I wake up earlier than I otherwise would have, because I am now responsible for getting these materials to the other workers of the promotion. I go to a Corner Bakery Cafe and spot the other three people. They are right on time, like most promotional workers tend to be. Maybe I should have been twenty minutes late like most supervisors in the promotion world, just to mess with them. I proceed to distribute the cards evenly and give people their shirts. We separate and head towards the Taste of Chicago, which is like a zoo with humans.

There are already thousands of people here and the temperature is soaring. This will be a three-day gig—Friday, Saturday, and Sunday. The goal is to get rid of these reward cards by the end of the weekend. I am partnered with a man in his forties. He is scrawny and spends several minutes spreading sunscreen all over his pasty white body. He is earnest and begins handing out cards immediately near the Buckingham Fountain. We decide it will be more efficient to separate, so I go a hundred feet away.

I take a look at the card. Buy six drinks at Caribou Coffee and get the seventh for free. The expiration date is two months from now. This may be the worst promotional offer I have ever seen: A short timeline during which someone has to buy several drinks to earn the free one—in the hottest months of the year. On the other hand, these cards probably cost next to nothing and I figure Caribou is just trying to get its name out there.

I begin to step in front of people, forcing them to take a card. Many people believe it is a voucher for a free drink at Caribou. This is probably because I am yelling, "Free Caribou Coffee!" and then very quietly, "reward card."

Like similar promotional gigs, we were told via email that we will be paid for four hours, but if we do an exceptional job and get rid of the cards ahead of schedule, we can leave early but still get paid for the full duration. I imagine a pile of Caribou Coffee cards at the bottom of a garbage can and me going home three hours early. Too soon. I have to make at least a little bit of an effort because right now, I am the supervisor—kind of.

"Free coffee?" someone asks me as they walk by.

"Sort of. If you buy six drinks, *then* you get your seventh for free. Awesome, right?" Unconvinced, he hands it back to me and continues to walk down the street.

I go at it for an hour and decide I should take a walk and check out the Taste. This is one of the biggest events in the city, although this year's version is different. Instead of booking big musical acts like previous years, they are featuring groups from the Midwest, both to save a lot of money and to promote local artists. The city also slashed four weekend festivals from the annual lineup and will instead incorporate them into the Taste. These are: Viva Chicago, Celtic Fest, Gospel Fest, and Country Fest. I think everyone agreed that was the smart thing to do. However, vendors at the Taste have been up in arms about the city not booking a major act, saying it will significantly decrease the number of patrons.

I can't tell if there are fewer people here. I am walking about one mile an hour, and there are people packed from one side of the street to the other. I go to the corner where the other Caribou team has set up shop.

"How's it going guys?"

"Almost done. You?"

"What! Done with all three hundred of your cards? That's impossible."

She isn't joking. I stand around for a few seconds and watch people come up to ask *her* for cards. At my post, some people look as if they want to punch me in the face when I extend my hand out to them.

"Well, that's it. See you tomorrow." The two of them leave less than ninety minutes into the day. My partner and I definitely got the shaft on placement. I should have told her that we'll need to switch tomorrow since I am now sort of the lead on this project, but I don't care enough.

I grab some fish and chips and then chill in the shade. I don't know a lot of people who come to this festival, because most of them say it's dumb and attracts only suburban tourists. They seem to be on to something. There are dozens of families that look like they have come straight from a *Jerry Springer Show* taping. There are parents screaming obscenities at small children while trying to juggle a shitload of food. There are the obligatory groups of dudes wearing wife beaters and oversized baseball caps with the size stickers still on. These guys are usually smoking nonstop and seem to be on-site all day, walking back and forth. I decide I should probably get out of here as soon as possible.

I return to my area, where my partner is still dutifully handing out cards. I tell him that the other group is gone, and he can't believe it, so I develop a new strategy. Why give only one card out when these great reward cards could be used by everyone in the family? I start giving out two cards at a time, sometimes even three.

"What's that, a free drink?" a guy says.

*Something like that.*

I hand him a couple of cards and quickly move away so he doesn't start asking questions. I decide I've had enough. I can give out more tomorrow, but it's way too hot to be outside right now. I tell my partner I'm bailing and that I'll see him tomorrow.

---

The second day is very much like the first. I still haven't seen Fatma, the supposed lead on this gig. I have a sneaking suspicion that I won't see her, which is exactly what I would do if I were in charge. Today, I decide to start off with my two-cards-per-patron model right away. I'm no mathematician, but my stack of cards is definitely dwindling twice as fast.

I don't want to leave too early, so I hang out by a big Pepsi promotion. I see a couple of people there from the soymilk gig I worked two months earlier. Their job is to pour samples of Pepsi. I feel for them. There is an unending line waiting to get samples because it is so hot out, or maybe it's because people love Pepsi.

There is also entertainment at this promotion. The MC has started a freestyle dance battle between two kids that are probably about eight years old. One kid is just jumping around, but the other kid has obviously had some serious lessons. He is spinning around on his head and executing other difficult breakdancing moves. This is entertaining for a while, but I need to find some shade again. I go back by where the other two promoters were working, but they are gone. They must have finished even earlier today.

There is no music playing yet, so there is not much to entertain me. I try a chocolate-covered banana and watch different groups of people walk by. This job is definitely one of the easiest gigs I've ever worked. I can do anything I want right now, but there just isn't much to do, and I feel bad for my partner. I head back in that direction and tell him I am going to bounce soon. He still has tons of cards, so I help him with his stack for about fifteen minutes. I tell him there is a good chance I will not be on time tomorrow, depending on how late the Wimbledon final goes in the morning. Djokovic is playing Nadal. It could be a long, grueling match, but it's one that I have to watch. Djokovic is having a magical season, only losing once to Federer in the semifinals of last month's French Open. It could turn out to be one of the greatest seasons in the Open Era, and I have to see it live.

---

The final ends up being a bloodbath, and I am able to get to the Taste on time for the third and final day. Just like the last two days, I go aggressively in the first thirty minutes until my initial burst of energy runs outs.

Like tennis or any other sport, it's all about momentum. Once I get a couple people standing by me, and people see me giving them something, this attracts other people and so on and so forth. The hardest thing is getting people to take the cards in the first place. I have a natural aversion for soliciting strangers to take worthless things, so I am terrible at this.

Soon, I lose interest and start walking around again. Out of the blue, I spot a high school kid on the ultimate summer league team that I am captaining. I screw up his name, but he still says he will hook me up with food. It turns out that he works at one of the stands every year. I follow him, and he gets me a potato pancake with applesauce on top. He has to get back to work, so I continue to wander. I check out one of the stages where somebody is playing. No good. I need to finish this gig once and for all.

I still have cards, but decide against handing them out. For the first time while walking around, I spot dozens of cards on the ground. People have apparently realized the cards are worthless. I don't know why they can't throw them in the trashcan, and decide that I shouldn't give any more away for the environment's sake.

I talk to my partner one last time and discover that he is a pretty interesting character. He has worked all over the world in banking. Now, he is trying to run his own social media business and is doing miscellaneous gigs like this in the meantime. I tell him it's been good working with him, and we part ways.

In total, I have been here for six hours over the last three days, which is half the amount of time I will get paid for. I never do see Fatma. Maybe this means I did a good job filling in as supervisor, and may have management potential in the promotional world. I shudder at this thought and head home to watch some tennis highlights.

# SEGWAY OR THE HIGHWAY

I know exactly how Christopher Columbus felt when he arrived in the Americas; the way he felt when the natives looked at him like he was an alien from a distant planet. I didn't have to cross an ocean to experience this. I didn't even have to leave my city. I was just five miles from my apartment and in the middle of one of the most dangerous neighborhoods in the country. I wasn't stared at because I was the only white person in the area, but rather because I was riding a Segway through the streets. I wore a bright blue Walmart shirt, and the Segway was decked out in Walmart signage. Never mind that it was 2:00 p.m. in middle of a Tuesday afternoon. There were hundreds of people hanging out all over the place and all of them had their eyes on me. School *was* out for the summer.

---

Once again, I had replied to a Craigslist ad and received a response a few days later saying I would be part of the team. I didn't know what I would be doing or what I would be promoting. I only knew that all of the specifics would be revealed at a meeting on Chicago's South Side two days before the five-day gig.

On the designated day of the meeting, four of us showed up as the young manager, Ed, arrived with some paperwork. Moments later, we were told that we would be cruising around on Segways promoting a new free shuttle being offered by Walmart for the neighborhoods on the West Side. After the paperwork, we would practice riding the Segways.

I was the first one to jump on the Segway and almost fell over as I struggled to balance myself. The others looked on in amusement as I teetered back and forth and drove around in circles. The key is to not lean too far forward or backward. Gradually, I got the hang of it and after a couple minutes, Ed declared that I was good enough for now. The others took their turn and we were done. Twenty minutes, but paid for two hours. Not bad, Ed.

———————

Two days later, I arrive at the meeting point, a Walgreens parking lot at Fullerton and Central. A truck arrives and Lenny, the driver, gets out to unload the Segways. We jump on and pose for a picture, all lined up in our Walmart shirts. Moments later, the Walgreens manager runs out and screams at us to get out of his parking lot. Ed tells us that that is our signal to go, and we take off. We start rolling down the street as crowds begin to gather along the road to stare at us.

"Whatcha doing?" people ask as we fly by.

We stop and hand them fliers explaining that there is a brand new shuttle system that does a route around the area, picking up people and taking them to the Walmart on North Avenue. There are six stops on the route and it is free. I get many chances to practice my Spanish, as eighty percent of the neighborhood is Latino. People are very receptive to the promotion, and nearly everyone enthusiastically takes a flier.

Ed pulls up in his car to tell us that we need to separate so we can cover more area. This is fine with me because I want to start exploring.

North of where I'm at is the Latino area and a neighborhood in the midst of gentrifying. To the south would be considered ghetto. By ghetto I mean high unemployment, low-income households, garbage-covered streets laden with potholes, high violent crime and murder rates, no museums or cultural spots, no grocery stores, numerous fast food restaurants, and hundreds of boarded-up homes.

I turn my Segway to the south. I won't have many opportunities to explore these streets with an actual purpose. Within moments, I turn off a main road and head straight into the heart of the neighborhood. I immediately attract an enormous amount of attention.

"Whatcha doing over there?"

"What is that thing?"

"Whatchu givin' out?"

"Come over here. What you got?"

I oblige their requests and give my spiel. I tell them that I'm not giving out anything—I am informing the local populace of the new shuttle Walmart is offering. Many people are visibly disappointed that I am not giving anything away. I continue to scoot around, drawing hoards of kids out of the woodwork.

"Can I ride that thing?"

"That's crazy!"

"Where you comin' from?"

I eventually roll my way back to the main street, stopping at bus stops, a logical place to talk to people. Every single car that goes by slows down. Several even stop to take pictures with their cameras and yell out the window in amazement.

It becomes clear that many of these people haven't been to downtown Chicago in recent years, which is only seven miles to the east. Downtown, one of the most popular tourist activities is the Segway city tour. On any given day, there are hundreds of them rolling around checking out Millennium Park and the lakefront. However, we are nowhere near downtown. The only body of water nearby is a small pond in a local park that is filled with garbage. Instead of the *Bean* and other city-commissioned artwork, there is brightly hued graffiti on the walls of abandoned buildings and fireworks detritus littering the streets left over from the Fourth of July festivities.

A few minutes later, I look down and notice my Segway only registers two bars of energy. I text Ed, and he tells me to go chill at the drop-off point, a good two hours before the job is supposed to be done for the day. I ride to a strip mall at a major intersection and hang out. As people come up to me and ask questions, the mall cop pulls up and asks if I can help him.

"Help you?" I ask.

"What are you doing?"

"Nothing. Just hanging out."

"Well, hang out somewhere else or there will be problems."

Okay, maybe I will check out that park across the street. I put the Segway down and hang out next to a pond, watching crawdads scramble along rocks underneath plastic bags and empty soda cans. Eventually, it is time to rendezvous so I head back. We fill out some paperwork, return our Segways, and head home.

------------

The next day, Ed says we need to go in pairs. "I just realized we are not in the greatest area, so you need to stay together at all times."

This proves to be a major nuisance. I am paired up with a woman named Jane, a little younger than me, who recently had a kid. She seems halfway intelligent until we get to the subject of directions. She had already explained how she barely found the meet-up point today because she "gets so lost all the time."

"Well, where are you from?" I ask.

"Here. Grew up in Chicago all my life."

*Hmmmm.*

Chicago is by far the easiest city to navigate in the world. Streets only go east–west and north–south. Main streets are every half mile in four block increments. 400 West. 800 West. 1200 West. 400 North. 400 South. So simple. Days earlier, I had shown around a Tunisian friend who was in town. He was a Chicago navigational expert before he had been in the city a day.

I now find myself partnered with the most directionally-challenged human being in history.

Ed tells us to go down to Division.

She looks at me and asks, "Where's that?"

I try to keep calm. "Are you joking?"

Twenty-six years she's lived in this city. I am getting frustrated. My brain is unable to register this. I want to ask her how she gets around, how she gets places, how she *lives*. I know four-year-old children who could find their way home in Chicago if they were given an address.

"I just don't know what the north and south mean and all of those numbers."

Someone kill me for this Segway and end this. I start explaining to her the simplicity and beauty of a grid system.

"Yeah, my dad has always tried to explain it to me. I just don't get it."

We go south on Central Avenue from Fullerton to Division. We take a right on Division and go a few blocks. I look at my phone.

"Looks like Ed forgot to give us fliers, so we need to meet back on Fullerton."

"Where is that?"

*How are you still alive?*

We had gone in a line and taken a right. To get back to where we started, we need to take a right and go back up the line. We had been gone for three minutes. I try to calm down and forget about it, but I just can't let it go.

"So streets go north–south and east–west. If a street has a W in front of it, it means we are on the west side. If it has an E, it means we are on the east side. So you know we are on the west side, right?"

She replies in the affirmative.

"So, that is what the W means."

"Ooooohhh. That's cool."

I think we have made progress until later in the day when she says she doesn't know how to get back to the truck, which is two blocks away.

"Jane, this is the street you drove in on, the one we have been on all day, the one where we always meet."

"Oh, I just get all mixed up."

Maybe she's genetically indisposed so it's fine that she can't find her way out of a paper bag. What's not fine is that she is clearly racist and says she won't go deeper into the neighborhoods, forcing us to stay on the main roads where there is exhaust in our faces, loud cars rushing by, and absolutely no shade from the midday sun. I can feel my face burning despite all the sunscreen I have applied.

"I just won't go anywhere near the houses. I fear for my life right now."

*Okaaay.*

It's bad, but it's not that bad. It's broad daylight and there are cops everywhere. What we do agree on is that hanging in a park is a good idea. I grab an ice cream cone from a peddler and sit at a bench. During our brief break, I discover that Jane graduated with an anthropology degree from a school in North Carolina. She has been doing this promo stuff ever since she graduated five years ago. She then talks about how she and her fiancée own their own business. I choose not to express my disbelief.

She explains that she has partnerships with all of the major mobile service carriers, as well as the major utility, Internet, and cable companies. She finds people deals and then gets a cut of the customer payments each month. I nod my head and smile while she elaborates on the finer points of her great business.

*So you do these gigs for fun? Your company must be booming.*

I tell her that when I need a cell phone, I go to a cell phone store and get one. I am confused by what she does, but don't really want to know how it works. I am just glad to be in the shade. After resting for a while longer, we get up and make our way back to sign out.

---

It's now day three, and Jane and I are back at it. I decide to see what the shuttle is all about. I navigate us to one of the stops and wait to see if it actually comes when it's supposed to.

Let's see, we're at Grand and Pulaski. Five after the hour, every hour. I glance at the time. 1:03. Okay, got a few minutes here. We find some shade across the street. 1:10. Still no shuttle. Nice work, Walmart. 1:15, still no shuttle. We cruise away.

Since I'm with Jane again, this means exploring the neighborhoods is off-limits. Still, I do have one weapon at my disposal. She never has any idea where she is. So I go off to find parts of the city I have only read about. We coast to the Central Green El station at Lake Street. It is 11:00

in the morning and there are *tons* of people hanging out on the corners, smoking cigarettes and killing time. They have nothing to do and nowhere to go. This is their life, and it is eye-opening. I have read many articles about the growing economic disparity all over the country and am seeing a perfect example in my city. One could be mistaken for thinking Chicago's economy is in great shape by walking through the Loop and seeing all of the white-collar workers entering skyscrapers. But out here and in numerous other parts of the city, there is nothing but idleness and poverty.

Then the shouts begin.

"Get over here. What'chu got?"

"Afternoon, sir. There's a new shuttle service running to Walmart. Hit. It. Up."

We will later find out that there is a large mental institution nearby, which would explain the erratic residents of the area. We do find a nice fountain in a small square and take a twenty-minute break. Jane talks about two other gigs she has later in the day.

"So 640 N. LaSalle. Is that close?" Please. Get me. Away from her.

I decide to give her a break from these neighborhoods and head west, to Oak Park. On the way, a guy toting a Whole Foods bag talks to us. "You guys better watch yourselves in that area. Not a good place to be."

After a few blocks, it's as if we have crossed over from Baghdad to Paris. There are sushi restaurants, lush green parks, a huge high school football stadium, and rows of well-kept houses. It is unbelievable. Just blocks away, there is a run-down ghetto, and now we are in yuppie central. Suddenly, no one wants the fliers. People here don't shop at Walmart. It is bad for communities, they say.

Jane loves it here, so we stop to grab a snack at a Dominick's grocery store. We get a text from Ed asking where we are, so I name another place back east since we are currently out of the zone we should be patrolling; Chicago Avenue and Austin Boulevard, which is the end of the line for the Chicago Avenue bus. There is a turnaround area, so we do tricks on our Segways and hand out fliers. The lights turn green, but people keep stopping to ask us what's going on, infuriating drivers behind them. We shout over a symphony of honking cars that there is a new bus shuttle available to Walmart.

It is only 3:00 p.m., but the other woman in our group has to go, so Ed says we can all go. We return, putting one more day in the books.

---

Day four is the most interesting. I am paired with the other woman, Rae, a native Israeli who has lived in Chicago for a year. She spends the first hour venting about spending the last two days with the other guy, Ivan. She says he goes all over the place and calls everyone friend and tells every black person he sees that they look like Dave Chappelle. She says she is over it, and we discuss where to drive our Segways. I discover that she is game for exploring. We immediately head into the side streets of Garfield Park[6]. Consistent with the past couple of days, we immediately attract dozens of people.

A man grabs fliers from us while his mom, an elderly woman sitting on a stoop screams, "Get me two! No. Three!" She thinks we are giving out coupons.

Then we come up to a group of teens. After we are done handing out fliers, one of them steps in our way, brandishing a huge stick.

Rae tells him to get out of the way.

*Uh oh.*

"Why don't you say please," he says.

*All right, I think we should go.*

"I said get out of the way," Rae says again, more forcefully. I now remember that she is from Israel and grew up with bombs exploding in restaurants on a regular basis. She drives around him, and he slams the stick against her Segway.

"Excuse me," I mumble as I go by. I look back and see the kid walking across the street, slamming the stick on the ground.

---

6 Garfield Park is a neighborhood on the West Side of Chicago hit hard by the housing crisis and is regularly in the news for violent crime.

Other than the angry teen, most people are very kind and keen to find out what our story is. This may be the only time they'll ever see people riding Segways in their neighborhood.

We continue to head south, and things turn a little ominous. A man asks us what we are doing in the neighborhood and warns us that we should be careful. We nod and continue our trek. As we pass Chicago Avenue and Pulaski Road, my memory clicks with why this intersection sounds familiar. A day earlier, I read about three violent robberies at gunpoint that had occurred in this vicinity within a twenty-four-hour period. We keep going down the rabbit hole. When we arrive at Madison Street and Pulaski Road, we have officially reached the epicenter of the neighborhood. There are hundreds of people milling about. We hand someone a flier as dozens of women charge at us to get in on the action.

A woman weighing at least 400 pounds in the passenger seat of a car in a fast food parking lot screams, "Come over here! What you got!"

I roll over. "Oh, we're just promoting this thing."

She is extremely disappointed and gets back to her fried chicken.

A teen with glazed eyes stumbles up and points at the Segway. "Let me ride it."

I laugh awkwardly and say we can't do that.

He responds, a little more forcefully this time, "Let me ride it."

"I'll get in trouble," I say.

He puts his hand on it, so I motion to Rae that we need to mobilize. We scoot forward, and as I look back, I see the teen in the street looking for cigarette butts to smoke.

The sugar-water peddlers are out in numbers on the street, braving the ninety-degree heat and trying to make a few bucks in the shadow economy. This is the first time I am legitimately concerned for my safety. People with no teeth or completely rotten teeth come up and grab for the fliers. Many are wearing clothes that clearly haven't been washed in weeks, which makes me feel incredibly displaced. We continue south to Jackson Boulevard and then Congress Parkway where *everyone* is paying attention and yelling at us, trying to figure out what is up. I decide to take a right and go into the neighborhood. Once again, it is a weekday afternoon, but no one seems to be working. As we pass houses, we see many instances of a dozen people hanging out on the porch, drinking beer and talking.

People pop out of windows and scream, "Walmart!"

Another dilemma has sprung up. We have no more fliers. On one hand, it is an excuse to ignore these calls and keep moving, but at the same time, we have no freebies to please the masses. The sidewalk is overrun with weeds, so we venture into the middle of the street and make it back to Cicero Avenue.

A police car rolls up to us and stops, making traffic go around it. The cop says, "Hey guys, what are you doing here?"

*Promoting this shuttle . . .*

"Do you know what neighborhood you are in? Stay on the main road and get out of here."

*Sounds good.*

We go a little bit north and take a short break by a bus stop. There is garbage strewn all over the place, including a twelve-ounce can of grape soda speared on the fence. I get close and check the label. Forty-eight grams of sugar[7].

We hit the road again and continue to get bombarded by people telling us they want a ride or for us to get off so that they can try. We politely decline and keep moving. Cars continue to stop, nearly causing accidents, only to find out that no, we are not handing out gift cards to Walmart.

We receive our fifth or sixth warning of the day from a man standing on a corner. "Y'all better get out of the hood before you get yourself robbed. People won't think twice 'bout robbin' those things and sellin' 'em."

Duly noted. We keep going north until I hear a loud crash accompanied with kids laughing. I look back and see Rae on the ground; her Segway has flown into the street and fallen over. She had jumped off because she thought she was going to fall. After getting back on, she tells me about how her mom never wanted her to ride a bike because she thought they were too dangerous. So at the age of twenty-eight, she still has never learned to ride a bike.

---

7 See "The Fats and the Curious"

It is time to meet at the truck and I am ready to head home. It has been a long, hot, intense day.

---

Day five. Finally. The Segway was fun the first few days and I have seen a lot of neighborhoods and talked to a lot of people, but I am anxious to end this gig. We have a limited number of fliers today, so I know we will be done early.

Today, Ed tells us we can go wherever. He needs a couple pictures of the girls handing out fliers, so he pairs Ivan with me. I find out a few minutes later why the girls despise him.

I am not sure if he is mentally disturbed, crazy, or just weird. He mumbles nonsense constantly and waves at people that aren't there. He will periodically go into the street for no reason and get in the way of traffic, completely oblivious to nearly causing accidents. He had been thirty minutes late yesterday with no explanation and when asked by Ed why he was late, he incoherently muttered something. When asked why he didn't text that he would be late, he said his phone wasn't working. Flaky McGee. Every other block, he tells me he has a friend that lives right by here or owns a place right over there. I tell him we are nowhere near the street he has mentioned and he doesn't care. We are on the far West Side, and when we stop occasionally to hand out the fliers, he gives random people a pitch about the events he is organizing and tells them they should come to Wrigleyville for a great time. "Celebrities, music, girls, it's going to be uh-*mazing.*"

"Okay, cool," say dozens of people that will never see Ivan again.

He drives by yelling out, "Cool!" and "Yeah!" to no one in particular. When asked about specific stops the shuttle makes, he gives outlandishly wrong responses, and I scramble to correct him. He is, however, down for hanging in the same park I had discovered the first day. I get some ice cream from another peddler, and we sit by the pond and watch a man and his kid fish. I scoot my way over, and the kid tells me they have caught two fish and a lobster.

A lobster?

I look in the bucket; it is a good-sized crawdad. Close enough.

After a lengthy break, we head to the Polish neighborhood, which is a completely different world than from the previous day. Manicured lawns, bakeries, nice churches, and well-dressed youth. We ride through a few parks and eventually make it to Diversey Avenue.

We find another park where I make my way across the baseball diamond. I realize too late that I am kicking up an immense amount of dust, and the wind is taking it right into the face of a guy lying on the grass nearby. He covers his face, and I apologize. Seconds later, Ivan begins to do wheelies and careens left and right on his Segway, kicking up even more dust as I scream at him to stop. The poor guy ends up with a dust storm in his face before Ivan hears me. I apologize again, and then head over to the basketball court to watch a pick-up game. I would not have been comfortable doing this where we were yesterday, but this is a very safe spot next to the Metra train line.

Ivan continues to spout nonsense, and I turn my brain off.

I glance at my watch. 2:00 p.m. About an hour left. We get up and bomb down Pulaski. Ivan alerts me that he is down to one bar of energy. Not a good thing, since we are still two or three miles from the rendezvous point. We slow down to save energy.

We are back in the area where people yell at us from their cars, but I no longer care and keep going. We make the final turn and see the truck in the distance. We load our Segways and I impatiently wait for the two girls to get back. Why are they always late? And how do they get lost so easily? We have come to this same spot five days in a row. Much to our chagrin, Ed makes us wait for them. When they finally arrive, we fill out the paperwork one last time, and that is it. Ivan tells me that he is running some events this summer and would like me to jump on board.

"Cool," I lie. "I think I have your number from the email."

Ivan is satisfied with my response, and I bolt across the street and jump on a bus, leaving behind neighborhoods I may not see again for a long time.

# SUBSTANCE ABUSE RECLUSE

I am packed into a small conference room with twelve other people, and we are all looking up at a flat screen monitor. This is a group interview for a telephone interviewer position with a policy research firm. The two women on the screen are on the East Coast, and I struggle to understand their thick New Jersey accents.

"All right, we've talked enough. Let's go around the room and hear a little about you guys—your name, your background, whatever you feel like saying."

A woman in her sixties starts us off.

"Well, my name is Janice. I was recently laid off as a school librarian and then my husband passed away soon after."

There are a few seconds of awkward silence. One of the interviewers on the screen says she is sorry. Janice continues and says she would like to get out of the house and do something different. She has been making documentary films and is looking to get a job on the side.

Next up is a man named John. He was laid off from a major technology firm a few weeks earlier. He was an executive in product development and used to travel to Asia on a regular basis for high-level corporate meetings. He has an MBA from Northwestern's Kellogg School of Business and speaks eloquently about his desire to learn more about the process by which government policy comes about. He mentions that he volunteers at a local museum, and it is clear that he is way too qualified for a ten dollar per hour position at a small call center.

Next up is a girl named Amanda. She is working on her PhD in Economics.

*You have to be kidding me.*

She wants a part-time job to complement her role as a teacher's assistant at a local college. She talks about her desire to understand how data is gathered and used through first hand experience.

This goes on for another twenty minutes. One woman was laid off as a mortgage analyst at a major financial institution and has her MA in Public Policy. Another one is working towards her law degree. One guy is a Northwestern University graduate and recently returned from travelling around the world for a year. He is looking for part-time work while he gets his MA in African Studies. Another guy just graduated with a degree in Economics from the University of Chicago. Someone is out of place here . . . and it's me. And maybe that one person who got up and walked out about twenty minutes ago.

It is my turn to talk. I had zoned out and didn't know we had to talk for five minutes about how we want to change the world, so I say that I am here because I happen to have a little experience getting yelled at by strangers on the phone. My background is in accounting and I really need a job. I think about making up something about how I am working on a graduate degree of some sort and intend on running for public office, but I choose not to.

"All right," the ladies say from the monitor. "We have a great group of candidates here. We'll get back to you guys shortly."

We all shuffle out.

A couple days later, I get a call, and am offered the job. I accept. There will be four days of training and a mandatory one-hour session for filling out paperwork.

I have just one problem. On the day I'm supposed to fill out the paperwork, I'll be in the middle of a gig where I ride a Segway around the most dangerous neighborhoods in Chicago[8]. I call to explain and they make a big deal out of it, saying it could jeopardize my employment, but

8 See "Segway or the Highway"

they make an exception and let me come in a little earlier. The paperwork takes me five minutes to fill out. Crisis averted.

---

At training, it is all the same people, so it looks like they hired everyone. The training is excruciatingly boring. We are each given a 500-page book and we go through the survey we'll be conducting. It is a survey about substance abuse treatment facilities throughout the country. We basically just call up these places and ask them about what they do and how many people they serve a year. This information goes into an annual directory that the government uses. For everyone else at training, this information is new and requires their rapt attention, but for me, I just try hard to stay awake. Since I had a job a few months earlier doing surveys for the CDC, I know how the process works.

To make the training more interactive, the instructors have us go through the survey. One of them acts as a hypothetical respondent while we take turns reading the questions to learn the content of the survey. None of us are able to pronounce varenicline or buprenorphine, so we practice together and say them over and over.

"If you guys stumble over these words, you aren't going to last long here."

There are a million possible things that can happen during a survey, and one woman in the group decides to ask about every single one.

"What do we do if the respondent says they already did the survey and sent it in a few days ago, but we haven't received it and . . . " Blah blah blah.

The instructors do their best to answer. Then it becomes a pattern. Every few minutes, her hand shoots up.

"Let's say that hypothetically speaking . . . "

*Here we go again.*

Every training session must have a person like this. She doesn't realize that we might actually get out early if she just shuts up. I want to tell her that for each of her million scenarios, we will cross those bridges when we come to them. She has a notebook and frantically writes the answers down to every question. I don't even have a pen with me.

The only good thing to happen during training is when a fire alarm goes off. We stop what we're doing and wait for it to run its course. Over the speakers, they announce that there is no fire and that people should stay in their offices so there isn't chaos in the stairwells. The problem is that the alarms are still going and are incredibly loud and are hurting my ears. I put my noise-canceling earphones on, but they don't help at all. After thirty painful minutes, the noise stops, and we resume our intense learning.

———————

I arrive for our first real day, and everyone is excited. Some of us are working the morning shift and the rest, the afternoon shift. I think back to the time I did my very first call at the CDC job. I didn't know how to change the volume and pressed the wrong key. The person hung up on me. Now I feel like a savvy veteran and am not nervous at all. This survey is much better than the one at the other gig. These people *want* to do the survey since it benefits them by allowing the facilities to be included in the directory. It's for a good cause, or at least that's what they tell us.

Just like the other job, we are constantly monitored. There are two monitors and they couldn't be more different. One day, I get a tap on the shoulder. It's Andrea.

"Hey, I was just listening to you on that call. You want to come to the office?"

I follow her into a room, and she goes down the list of things she recorded.

"You were nice and clear on the phone. Very polite. Didn't read the entire question a couple times, but no big deal. Got a complete. Good work. Just sign here."

I am out of there in less than two minutes. Andrea monitors me about fifteen times over the three-month gig, and this is how it goes every time.

Then, there is Damon. He is a nice guy, but is a little more on edge and is a perfectionist.

I get done with one of the more frustrating calls I have had so far. I'm not even sure the woman was speaking English, as I had to repeat everything, and her responses made no sense. I felt I was being as polite as possible. I hang up and feel a presence behind me. Damon, and he's glaring at me.

"Let's go to the office."

*What's the problem?*

He closes the door, turns to me and says, "What the hell was that?"

"What do you mean?"

"That interview. That was a disaster. Was that a joke? It didn't even seem like the same person I have listened to over the past few weeks. I actually wasn't doing an official monitoring session. Otherwise, I would have given you a zero."

I am feeling pretty uncomfortable. "I thought it went well, given the circumstances."

Apparently, we both think the other is joking. He goes through the survey and talks about how I was leading the respondent, which is a big no-no in this world. I tell Damon that if I ask a question three or four times and can't get a real response, then I need to move on or I am going to lose the survey. He disagrees. We must protect the integrity of the information. He says I talked too fast and was making the respondent uncomfortable with the pace. This goes on for fifteen minutes, and I am out of there, hoping Andrea does my next monitoring session.

---

Like my last job as a telephone interviewer, people figure out pretty quickly if the gig isn't for them. The guy getting his MA at Northwestern is gone after two days. The PhD candidate is gone after a week. Two other people disappear a couple weeks later. It is down to about six of us from the original group, plus two others who worked the survey last year. One of them is a guy in his forties who sounds incredibly sarcastic and reads everything in its entirety including the introduction, which takes about a minute. Whatever he is doing, it is working. He is getting tons of surveys done.

There is a guy next to him who has been here for a while as well, but he is working on a different survey. He *is* the most sarcastic person I have ever heard in my life. He is also the slowest speaker I have ever heard. And, he somehow manages to complete survey after survey. He never breaks his cadence, never hurries, and never gets flustered, even when it's obvious that the person on the other line wants to hang up.

"It is a very important survey, ma'am. We would very much like your . . . I understand ma'am. But this is a very important survey. Oh. I understand, but this is a very important . . ." He wears down the person on the other end completely, and then proceeds with the survey.

The former executive, John, turns out to be one of the best interviewers. He gets promoted to what is called a refusal converter. When people say they don't want to do the survey, we click an option listing the facility as a refusal. John's job is to call them back to try again, which is not a job I would want.

One of my favorite memories of John's work occurs towards the end of the data collection period. First of all, one has to understand that the survey takes anywhere from 20–30 minutes in its entirety. He calls the listed number and launches energetically into his spiel.

"I understand you talked with Rupert earlier but weren't willing to do it. We certainly understand your concern . . . Oh. You don't have time. Well certainly, sir, yeah, oh yeah, that is definitely a consideration. Well, I will tell you what. We can start and stop at your leisure, since this is a very important survey. Oh, you don't have time *and* you don't want to do it. Can you remind me why you don't want to participate in this very important survey? Very good. Certainly, yeah, yeah, very good, sir. Well yeah, I know how you might not think there are benefits for you, but there's more to it than that."

If I told somebody that the survey wasn't about them and to stop being selfish, I would have been fired, but this guy has a way of sounding so earnest that it works.

"A lot of people use this information and it can really have an impact on your local communi . . . Oh, you still don't want to do it."

I would have hung up minutes ago.

"Like I said, we could always start and see how far we get. Oh. You don't believe in it. And that's certainly understandable."

I can't believe what I am listening to. It is like a real-life Ned Flanders. I had stopped dialing minutes ago to listen to the magic happening. After about fifteen minutes, the same amount of time in which the survey could have been completed, the guy hangs up.

No survey. I can't stop laughing at how ridiculous the call was.

John gets up and reflects on the call. "The guy was incredibly patient and kind . . . he just really didn't want to participate."

The former librarian is my next favorite interviewer. Even after a couple of months, she struggles with the survey computer program and always gets lost and presses the wrong buttons.

"Wait a minute, ma'am. I did something crazy. I don't know where I'm at. I apologize . . . Oh, okay, where are we again?"

I cringe. It typically takes her about forty-five minutes to do a survey, compared to everyone else's twenty. Still, she has stuck it out with the rest of us.

———————

Towards the end of data collection, we have called many of the numbers upwards of twenty or thirty times. There are so few facilities left in the sample that we start calling many of them two or even three times a day.

I pull up one file and read the notes on the potential participant. Hmmmm. We have called her about fifteen times. Over a month ago, the respondent said she sent in the hard copy. We called her a week after that and told her we never received it. So she sent it in again, and now it is three weeks after that, and it still hasn't arrived. The notes say that she is adamant she has sent it in twice and absolutely refuses to do it over the phone since she did it herself. This should have been coded as a refusal.

I ask Damon how to handle this one. Just throw it back in the pile and let someone else handle it? He says to do whatever. I decide I will take one for the team, and I dial.

She begins ranting immediately. "I thought you guys might be calling again. And I'm actually glad that I'm not busy right now so that I can let you have a piece of my mind."

I don't get to say a word for the next ten minutes.

"You work for the worst organization I have ever come across. You guys are worthless and incompetent and couldn't do something right if your lives depended on it."

I look for a speakerphone option but can't find one.

"I sent it in TWICE, PRIORITY MAIL! So if it's lost, it's YOUR FAULT! There is a post office next door, and I walked it there MYSELF. And you know what? I used to believe in this survey, but last year I WASN'T EVEN PUT IN THE DIRECTORY! I spent all that time doing the survey and I WASN'T EVEN PUT IN! Every single one of you is worthless. I can't believe your organization is still in business. You guys are a joke. I don't want to be called again this year for this survey. And you know what? I never want to be called again, EVER! Take our facility out of your records, out of your system, out of whatever, so I never hear from you guys again! You got that? Can you do that? Or will you screw that up too? You have a nice day."

"You have an awesome day, too, ma'am."

Click.

That phone call is the highlight of the three months I have been on this gig. I gather around the troops and tell them what just transpired. People agree that it sounds like the most out of control respondent yet, which fills me with pride.

---

It is about a week before the end of the survey. Like every day on my break, I walk out by the river, which is right next to our building. I look across the bridge and see that there is something going on. I walk over, and it is a huge promotion for United Airlines. People are waiting in line to walk up to a fake baggage claim to pick one from a wide variety of bags. Then someone opens your bag to see if you won anything. I am second in line. The man in front of me watches about ten different bags go by.

He chooses the biggest bag and screams, "That one!"

He reminds me of the character in *Indiana Jones and the Last Crusade* taking forever picking out the Holy Grail.

"Congratulations. You won one hundred United Airline miles!"

He chose . . . poorly.

I get up and point to the first bag that passes by. It is small and unassuming. A promotion staffer grabs it, glances inside, and then yells for the MC to come over.

"We've got a big winner here. 50,000 miles!" The MC yells this out over the speaker, and everyone claps and goes nuts. I also win two VIP passes to the lounge in the airport where you can eat and drink as much as you want before your flight. I am taken over to a table where I fill out the paperwork. I even receive a $400 gift card to pay the taxes on the prize, which is unusual for things like this. They ask me where I will go with my miles, and I tell them San Francisco. I am suddenly pleased that this random gig led to an unexpected stroke of luck.

---

It is the final day of data collection. Those facilities that don't respond will have another week to do the surveys online and then they will be left out.

It is apparently an annual tradition that everyone goes to a local bar to celebrate. We get drinks, and clink our glasses.

"To substance abuse!" I hope karma isn't a real thing. The lead supervisor downs about five pints in thirty minutes. He comes over to me.

"Man, you were the best. Man, you showed up *every* day. You never skipped out. That's *incredible*. Half the people quit, then everyone else called in sick every other day. Not you, man. Not you."

I thank him for the kind words.

"If you *ever* need a reference, man, I *got* you. I will talk you up big time."

I tell him I appreciate it.

He tells me this gig is just what pays the bills, but music is his true passion. In fact, he is a keyboardist in a rock band and writes his own scores.

Then Damon comes over. He swears every other word and talks about how he couldn't give a shit about the survey. The ex-librarian tells me she is orchestrating a huge anti-war protest the following weekend. We talk about baseball and other things besides drugs used to treat opiate addicts.

The guy who talks super slowly takes out a sheet of paper. He has spent the last three months writing down every funny name he overhears from other interviews. He reads through them, and we all laugh at the ones we remember, like Sandy Beaches and Michael Jordan. It is only eight o' clock, but we are going to call it a night. Or not. Apparently, the gang is going to another bar, but I politely decline.

It is nice seeing the crew outside of work for once, but I am going to a movie later at the Chicago International Film Festival. I say goodbye to everyone and head to the theatre, but have a feeling that I might see them again.

# MARIO MOB

I walk outside into the cold, windy weather, and rain slams into my face. I should be wearing a raincoat and wielding an umbrella, but instead, I must make do with long johns and a thin, long-sleeved T-shirt. I am headed towards downtown Chicago to take part in a flash mob promoting a new Mario Brothers video game. We will dress up in Mario costumes, and aren't supposed to bring anything with us because there will be no place to store personal belongings. They said the promotion was a big success in Houston and San Diego a few weeks ago, but I don't know why they opted to have Chicago's event in the middle of November, which is one of the coldest months of the year.

I get on the bus, and people give my outfit strange looks. The bus arrives at the station just as the train is pulling in. It is completely packed, but I choose to be the guy who squeezes in anyway. I am not going to wait outside in this weather for another seven minutes. I arrive early, so I chill in a mall near the meeting point. I text a friend, who is also doing the gig, and he swings by to hang with me. Neither of us has been told anything about the event, besides the fact that we will be dressed as cartoon characters. Supposedly, we will learn everything at the beginning of the promotion. For now, it's a glorious mystery.

We head back out into the elements and move towards a small park near the Museum of Contemporary Art (MCA) where a large group of people are milling around. I am on team one, and check in with a guy holding a big sign that has the number one on it. Off to a good start. There will be eight teams in total, each containing nine people. It is now 8:30 a.m., and the bigwig comes up to our team lead, Aaran.

"How many you have?" he asks Aaran.

"Five, including me."

"Call the others to see what's up and if they're not here in five minutes, they're out."

Aaran calls the four people. Two of them don't pick up and the other two say they will be here soon. Fortunately for these types of gigs, there are plenty of pocket shifts—that is, a group of people to fill in when others bail on their assignments.

The other two never do show up, which is surprising as the company running this promotion, much like others in the industry, charges a fifty dollar no-show fee. I can imagine those two guys getting a bill a few weeks later for a gig they never worked. They will go from being paid eighty dollars to owing fifty. Brutal.

We take two replacements and move to an open spot in the park. The bigwig comes up to our team with his clipboard in hand.

"You guys are team one, so you'll learn the dance first."

As eighty people look on, we are taught the dance we'll be performing later today. It is incredibly simple. Side step right, side step left, side step right, shake our booty, and raise our fist on four. Then we rotate ninety degrees and do it again. On the fourth part, along with the raised fist, we jump into the air.

"You guys ready to try it with the music?"

I guess so.

He cranks up the Mario music, counts us off, and we do our thing. Everyone learns the dance in about two minutes. One guy isn't comfortable and wants another run through, so we have to do it again, much to our chagrin.

Of the eighty-odd people in attendance, about ninety percent are male. The original requirement was that you had to be a guy less than five feet eleven inches. Apparently, there weren't eighty men available and willing to do this on a Wednesday morning, so they opened it up for taller guys and women.

My team is a pretty laid back assortment of characters. We have the obligatory hipster, wearing his tight jeans and rocking out to his iPod while we wait. There is another guy who looks like a Rocco or Bruno, and wouldn't be out of place as a hit man for the Chicago Outfit. We have one female in the group who laughs at everything and says she does gigs like this all the time. Our lead is named Aaran. Yes, there are three A's in his name. No one seems to be too excited about the event. I see two other people who I worked with on the Walmart Segway promotion. Jane, the directionally-challenged girl from that gig is not one of them. Or, maybe she was one of the people that never showed up for team one because she couldn't find the meeting point.

We have been here over an hour. I am freezing my ass off, but it looks like everyone has learned the dance and we are mobilizing. We walk across Michigan Avenue and go into a Hyatt Regency. Teams one and two follow a supervisor into a small hotel room where they have stored our costumes. We cram in and begin the transformation into a mass of Marios. It is a pretty legitimate costume—mustache, tail, ears, everything. We are Tanuki Marios, which was the raccoon suit introduced in *Super Mario Brothers 3* that allows him to fly.

We are ready to go, and meet down in the lobby with the other groups. We exit and immediately attract hoards of attention. People whip out their phones to take pictures and look on in bewilderment. Aaran said he forgot something and will be right back. He comes back and sheepishly announces that he doesn't have the map. Luckily, another lead has one, so he looks at it to figure out our route.

"Looks like we are going near the MCA, where we started."

I gather that all of the teams will go their separate ways until later in the day. Our job now is to give out cards that promote the new video game.

We arrive at the museum, and I realize that this is probably the part of downtown that has the *least* amount of pedestrian traffic. We huddle up as the wind hits our faces. Aaran checks the sheet.

"Okay . . . so we wait here until 11:00."

The hipster looks at his watch. "It's 10:15 . . ."

Fortunately, a museum security guard arrives and tells us that we are loitering, and to get off the property. I thank him silently as he walks off.

The new plan is to walk around, get rid of the fliers, and get people excited. People are definitely surprised at running into a band of Marios, and many want to take pictures with us. We walk over to Lake Shore Drive and as one car comes flying by, the passenger sticks his head out and yells, "Marioooooooooooo!!! Yeah!!!"

We circle back, return to Michigan Avenue, and see another group of Marios. They have a much better location because there are people walking by constantly. Another one of the supervisors is nearby and insists that we go back by the MCA. We do as we are told and go back to home base. I discover a bus stop with a Plexiglas cover that makes for a good wind blocker and hang out with people waiting for the bus.

When the occasional pedestrian walks by, we dance around and yell out in a cheesy Italian accent, "It's me! Mario!"

Some people are amused, but many are not. We offer the card to one man who just glares and says, "No."

We are also beginning to cause traffic problems, similar to when I was riding a Segway through the ghetto. One driver stops in the middle of the street to take a picture of us, triggering the person behind him to honk.

We are near Northwestern Hospital and I see a couple of doctors across the street. "Hey guys, get over here. We need your help. We have Mario fever!"

We make a lap around the same block several times. Aaran says it is time to meet back at the hotel. Since we are team one, we will meet team two, then together find team three, and so on. We walk back to where we started. There are a few teams there already, so we join them. We all yell and jump around wildly. It is a spectacle. Tourists hand their cameras to bellmen and jump in for a picture with thirty Marios. Aaran returns and says we need to go back to the MCA—he had misinterpreted the directions.

*Come. On.*

The wind picks up again and it begins to rain harder. Our team is quickly losing morale. We get back to the MCA, and Aaran looks around and asks where the hipster went. No one knows. Oh well. I don't blame him.

After another twenty minutes, it really *is* time for the show. We meet up with three other teams, bringing our gang to about forty people. I discover that my original team is by far the most laid back. Guys from the other teams are completely in character, talking just like Mario and running around like he does in the video game. They make jokes about needing some mushrooms and gold coins. Coincidentally, there was a flash *crime* mob in this exact neighborhood a few months ago. A large group of teens spontaneously attacked a few people, stealing things and beating people up before splitting off in different directions. I begin to wonder if some of these Marios had any connection to that incident.

We walk up Michigan Avenue where Greenpeace workers, tourists, Apple employees, and everyone else have taken notice of us. Aaran seems to have disappeared, so we do whatever we want. I am seeing the crowd effect first hand, and it is amplified by our ridiculous but highly recognizable costumes. The Mario suits are making people feel like they can get away with anything.

One dude starts break dancing on a corner while others run up to cars and dance around as the cars wait for the light. There are a couple of guys hitting on every girl that walks by our group. They refer to the girls as Princess Peach, and say that Mario is here to rescue them. A couple of Spanish women walk by, and one Mario asks for their número de teléfono to no avail.

We walk by an elderly man, and another Mario says, "What's up, old man."

Yet another Mario tells the Greenpeace workers that we are saving the Princess and the world at the same time, but they are not amused.

Eventually, we make it to the huge statue of Marilyn Monroe, a new art installation at Pioneer Square. Naturally, our mob goes up to it, and dozens of people immediately approach to take pictures with us. Several Marios get photos taken of them looking up her dress. I will appear anonymously in hundreds of random pictures on strangers' cameras from all over the world.

A hundred feet away, a seemingly professional camera crew is interviewing a man. I watch a group of Marios walk over and go behind the guy. The cameraman slowly rotates so they are no longer in the frame, but they move with him to get back on camera. He eventually turns it off, the interviewer yells at them to get out of there, and the Marios take off so there is no trouble.

Word gets to NBC (the studio is just a few steps away) of what is happening outside, and a representative pops out to interview us for a live taping, so we move over to the NBC tower. The meteorologist is live on the air, saying that when she went out for coffee, she saw dozens of Marios all over the place. One of the Marios gets interviewed because he seems to be the only one who knows anything about the video game we are promoting. Meanwhile, several Marios have walked away, and are talking on cell phones and sitting down. The team leads are worried because we are supposed to be at the Hancock tower at noon to do our dance—the original marquee event of this gig—but this impromptu TV time has thrown the schedule for a loop.

I look around, and one guy has moved his raccoon tail to the front of his body and is swinging it around suggestively. This is getting out of control.

Someone comes up to us and asks who we are.

"Mario . . . ever heard of him?"

Apparently not.

Later on, someone else asks us the same question and somebody replies, "Mickey Mouse."

Finally, a supervisor shows up and tells us that we have to roll and return to the Hancock Tower for our performance. We begin to walk back the same way we came. The vast majority of people we pass on the way smile and laugh at the ridiculousness of the scene. We continue and don't even stop at red lights. Why? Because we fucking can. We are above the law when we are video game heroes.

When we arrive, they tell us the performance has been done. The other half of the mob did it fifteen minutes ago. The show is over.

*Okaaaay.*

Even without knowing anything about the video game or the schedule, I could have done a better job organizing this gig if someone had given me five minutes, but it doesn't matter. It is freezing out, and it is time to go. We sign time sheets and are told we can keep the Mario outfit.

Sounds like I don't have to worry about my Halloween costume this year.

# A CORPORATE SURPRISE

After waking up at 5:15 a.m. on a Thursday morning, I pick up my buddy, Mike[9], and we head towards the suburbs. We were told by the marketing company to arrive at the site by 7:15. We pull in at 7:10 to find that we are the first ones here. Not long after, a man comes around the corner, introduces himself as Sahid, and tells us he flew in from Los Angeles to manage today's event. He can't believe how cold it is in Chicago in November. He says we may not be able to get into the place until 7:30 or 7:45, depending on the manager.

We are saved from turning into human icicles when we see that the door is ajar because the manager is already here, and we head inside. It is a beautiful, historic movie theatre that has a large auditorium with one screen. The manager is a woman in her sixties who says she has been hosting corporate events here for many years. We have some time to kill, so Mike and I explore the theater while the other team members gradually arrive.

There will be thirty of us in all, an even mixture of men and women, mostly in our twenties. We are all wearing business casual attire and some are even wearing business suits with ties. We will attend the quarterly meeting of a major corporation, and need to be able to blend in with the hundreds of shareholders who will be in attendance.

Sahid checks everyone off a list and takes us inside the theatre to brief us on today's assignment. A billion dollar corporation is having their shareholder meeting in this theatre in a couple of hours, and we are

9 Soymilk and Kickstarter Mike

going to liven things up by having a flash mob right in the middle of it. We will be placed sporadically throughout the theatre so that when the time comes, we will be surrounding the crowd.

"All right, I need three people to handle the big cannons—confetti cannons."

Several arms shoot up immediately. These people won't have to sit in the crowd, but will be situated under the stage waiting for their cue to pop out of trap doors and shoot confetti fifty feet into the air. Others will set off smaller cannons at each corner while another couple of people will run up and down the aisles with silly string. Everyone else will have signs and noisemakers.

He explains everything like he is planning a military operation. After assigning roles, we all go to our places for a quick run-through. They show the video that will be played towards the end of the meeting. About a minute into it, the words cheap, simple, and convenient run across the screen. Right after, it says: All around you. At that moment, we get up, blast cannons, make noise, and go crazy. It is supposed to accompany the presentation and wow the crowd. We do two takes and are good to go.

Before heading out to wait in the lobby, we ask Sahid what we should do if we end up sitting down and shareholders talk to us. He says we should be ourselves, but to make sure we don't mention that we are with a marketing company. Besides, he says, since they are shareholders, most people won't know each other anyway.

One of the company representatives that knows the plan overhears this and interrupts, "Who told you this is a shareholder meeting? This is an employee meeting for the three hundred Chicago workers."

*What?*

"So everyone will recognize that you don't work here, all thirty of you guys. But I work in marketing, and you can just say you are new to marketing."

*Hmmmmm.* We are supposed to be completely anonymous, blending in with other shareholders from around the country, but it turns out, everyone that will be here today works together on a daily basis. And, many of us in the flash mob have huge, conspicuous signs next to our chairs.

"One other thing," says the same marketing person. "Our company is known for its laid back culture, and we wear jeans and T-shirts to work. You guys will be the only ones dressed in nice clothes."

As a result of this news, a few of us start discussing what role we will play if confronted by actual employees. One guy says he will tell people he is the owner of the theatre and is just sitting in on the meeting for the heck of it. The rest of us decide to keep with the marketing idea. Unfortunately, there is a good chance that several of these people will *be* in the marketing department. If that happens, we will launch into a rant about a fictitious HR person, a guy who is always cranky and goes out for smoke breaks all the time.

We practice. "Yeah, you know the one. Never smiles. And have you seen this stuff about the Euro lately? The world is going to hell in a hand basket."

Anything to deflect suspicious people.

Mike and I talk to a couple other guys working the gig. One guy says he is an opera singer who has never actually sung in an opera, and is working as an actor and a butler. Wait, a butler? Apparently, he works in a mansion on the North Side of Chicago alongside gardeners, cooks, and nannies. The other guy just moved here two weeks ago from Boston. He studied business in college but will try to make it in the comedy world and has just begun taking classes at the famed Second City. He is entering the world of working shitty jobs with the hopeless dream of becoming a star.

Meanwhile, the team of supervisors decides that silly string is out because it is too messy. So now we are down to confetti cannons and noisemakers. We'll just have to make do.

———————

Some theatre workers arrive and make popcorn. Soda is served up, and a bus arrives with a load of employees, so Sahid tells us to head to our seats. We are all sitting on the ends, so we are able to jump out for the stunt without stumbling over people. I sit down and talk to the flash dancers nearest me. After a few minutes, I get up to go grab a soda. I return two minutes later, and my sign is gone.

*Uh-oh.*

A girl by me thinks a manager took it. I look in the row behind me to see that a woman who is not with the promotion has taken it and has put it in a seat with the message looking outward.

*Yeesh.* These signs are supposed to be as hidden as possible so people aren't privy to the flash dance. I walk over and tell the woman that it needs to go back to where it was, because the marketing people are doing something with it later. She had been using it to hold a seat for her friend but politely gives it up.

I leave again to throw my popcorn away, come back a minute later, and a different employee has taken my seat. I have not learned my lesson. I glance left and right, grab the sign, and quickly transfer it across the aisle to a different seat and stealthily slide into the row.

————————————

It is just about show time. I look around and make eye contact with various people, and it feels like something out of a spy movie. Nobody knows what is about to hit them. Someone has inflated a bunch of beach balls, and the crowd is knocking them all over the place. I get up, slam one back behind me, and tell a co-dancer that my mom would be so proud right now. She replies that she doesn't tell her mom that she is unemployed but rather that she works in marketing.

A woman gets up on stage and tries to get the crowd riled up.

"WHAT IS UPPPP! CAN I GET SOME NOISEEEE!"

These people have gotten out of the office for the day but aren't *that* excited.

She tries again. "COME ON NOW. YOU CAN BE LOUDER THAN THAT. LET'S HEAR SOME NOISEEEEEEEEE!"

This time the crowd does what it is told, if only to get the show moving. She says this is going to be an awesome quarterly presentation and gives the itinerary for the day.

First up is the CEO. He gives an immensely slow and boring summary of the quarter's earnings.

"Okay, you can see that revenue has shot up three percent from 2010 Q3. You know why? Because of all your hard work. Give yourself a round of applause."

The crowd cheers.

"You know we have to talk about it. We have to talk about the price increase. We thought long and hard, did test studies, everything. And the bottom line is, we had to do it. But we'll be stronger in the long run."

I look around and see dozens of employees playing games on their phones and texting. The CEO wraps up his portion of the meeting and heads to his chair. To keep the energy flowing, the MC gets back up and says we are going to have a little trivia contest.

"I am going to pick someone from the crowd to come up here and see if they know the answer. You. You there in yellow." I am wearing a yellow shirt, and she is looking in my direction.

*Shit.*

Suddenly, a man with a yellow shirt to my immediate left jumps out of his seat. He gets up, says his name, and is asked the question. He gets it right and gets his choice of three prizes: a certificate for a spa treatment, a dinner certificate, or whatever is in the MC's pants. This last option makes the crowd go wild. She has an envelope in her back pocket, and everyone laughs at her wording. People scream that he should take what is in her pants, so he does—a fifty-dollar gift card. The crowd applauds.

Now it is time for the CFO and founder of the company to deliver his speech. He says he only has two slides—instead of twenty—and the crowd goes nuts again. But he still manages to waste a lot of time telling anecdotes that people don't care about.

"Now people want to know what the latest is on the search for a new, full-time CEO as John is leaving us in a few months. We definitely want people with experience with a billion dollar company as well as experience with a fast growth organization like ours. BUT MOST IMPORTANTLY, they need to fit in with our culture. THAT has been the key to our success—our team atmosphere and passion for making the company better every day."

The crowd cheers.

He then shows a video of employees all over the country taking part in community service events. The company is committed to community service and gives paid time off to volunteer. He shows another video where people fill in the blank of this phrase: I am_____Because_____. The company encouraged people to make their own videos, inserting their own words. I am strong Because I have great employees around me. I am passionate Because I want to be a better person. I am here Because I am partaking in a flash mob and getting paid for it and have nothing better to do with my time.

The crowd is losing focus again, so the MC encourages everyone to get on their feet. I take the opportunity to hit up the bathroom so I can avoid doing whatever activity she has planned. The bathroom is packed, and people joke that there are only women left in the theatre right now.

When I return, the last speaker of the day is on the stage. She is the brand manager for the company. Her fifteen minutes on stage are absolutely cringe-inducing. She shows a statistic from a study the company had commissioned: four out of five people like having fun.

I look at Mike, and we try to hold it together. Brilliant work. This must have been a groundbreaking survey developed over many years.

But, she says, a lot of them can't afford to have fun, so it is vital that the company keep its prices low. Then she pauses before revealing the focus of the brand.

"Our company is FUN."

I look around and people are dismayed.

"So, I know what you guys are thinking. You have been working for months on this and that's it—we are fun?"

Actually, yeah, I imagine a lot of people are thinking that. I am also guessing that they are wondering why she has a job.

"It is so simple, that I probably don't even need to be on the stage."

Agreed—but she stays on for another ten minutes.

The next slide comes up, revealing the exciting conclusion to her presentation as she reads it aloud.

"It's a BIG deal." She leans back, crosses her arms, and nonchalantly continues, "Because it's not a big deal."

*Alriiiiiiiiiggght.* A college education, a director position in the company, several weeks of focused work, and this is what she came up with. A first-year marketing student could have come up with a better slogan. She moves on to explain potential new lines of business and ideas being mulled over internally.

It's just about time. She starts a video to summarize her presentation. It is the video with our secret words. Cheap. Simple. Convenient. Get ready . . . All Around You.

I jump up with the other flash dancers, and we go nuts. There is a song playing over the sound system while we jump up and down yelling random things. I pick up some of the beach balls and hurl them into the crowd. Some employees get up as well, thinking they should be standing just like us. The cannons go off without a hitch, the women run from the back of the theatre with noisemakers, and I hold my sign and wave it back and forth. There is confetti everywhere, and the crowd is stunned.

Then, just like that . . . we are gone.

We run out the back of the theatre.

I would like to leave now, but we are told that we must distribute boxes of candy that have some sort of play money attached. Mike and I immediately start talking about the brand manager's epic fail and are laughing uncontrollably. Some ushers tell us to shut up, so we try to keep it together. We finally get the signal to head back in. I am embarrassed to return to the theatre, but I diligently go row by row distributing the goods as the MC makes her final comments. I wonder if anyone in the crowd makes a connection between the part of the CFO's speech about cutting costs and the fact that their marketing department just spent $5,000 for a twenty-second flash mob at their quarterly meeting.

We thank Sahid and head outside where it is snowing. Mike and I are still laughing about the brand manager, which made the event worth it for both of us. I would have done this gig for free just for that part.

"Mike, this gig was a BIG DEAL, you know . . . because it wasn't a big deal, 'kay?"

# OOMPAH LOOMPA CHOCOLATE CHALLENGE

I get up on a Saturday morning after five hours of sleep. A couple days earlier, I had heard about a job fair at a local chocolate factory. It was for a month-long stint during the busy holiday season. I have to show up today for an hour if I want a chance at the gig. I arrive early, so I hang out in my car listening to music. I see people walk up from various directions and go inside the building. At five minutes until the hour, I walk inside to join the group.

A skinny kid, unshaven, and clearly not a fan of being here this early says, "You here for the chocolate thing?"

I say that I am.

"We're just going to wait here for about ten minutes and go up as a group."

People start to show up every few minutes. Since I am nearest the door, I open it for them.

"You here for the chocolate thing?" the guy asks everyone.

There are about twelve of us now, and no one says a word. Most of us are dressed in street clothes, but a couple people have worn nicer clothes and wield resumes. I thought this gig was for hauling boxes around, but I guess some people don't want to be unprepared.

Finally, after fifteen minutes, we are told to head upstairs. The skinny kid takes us through a labyrinth of doors and corridors. We see pallet after pallet of stacked chocolate slabs. There are people shuffling around wearing white aprons and hairnets, working the magical chocolate-making machines. It is chaos, as they are preparing for the busy season, which is why we are here. These people don't look nearly as excited as the Oompa Loompas in Willy Wonka's factory. This is probably because the place runs nonstop, and these people are just finishing the night shift. I know that feeling.

We are taken into the break room where a group of workers are eating their breakfast or lunch or dinner—who knows. We cram in. I find my way to the corner, and then a woman comes in. Is this the person we give our golden tickets to?

"Hi, I'm Natalia. I'm the one who emailed you guys. Welcome to the fair. It's going to be a good time." She says this with no hint of sarcasm.

First, we put our names on a sheet of paper that will serve as our report card for the day.

"All right, we will take three of you at a time and get this thing started."

*What exactly are we starting?* My name is called, so I am about to find out.

A young, hipster-looking guy gets up from a computer and explains our first test.

"On the table, you will see six different chocolate bars, including milk chocolate, almond, caramel, and a few others. I will give you a sheet of paper that is an example of an order document. When I say go, you will pick out your order and come back to me, and I will check your accuracy. Any questions?"

*Just one. Is this a fucking joke?*

"No questions? All right, here are your hypothetical orders . . . and GO!"

I look down and see three bars listed. One chocolate. One mint. One berry. I go to the table and pick up one of each and hand them to the guy.

"Five seconds! Nice work . . . and you got all the right ones."

*What can I say? I'm a fucking baller.*

The other two people are both successful, and we all score a passing grade. On to our next test.

"I am going to put these three boxes of chocolate on the table. When I say go, you will grab one at random and find which pallet it belongs to.

Put the box on the pallet and then figure out how many chocolate bars are on the pallet."

*How are we supposed to . . .* he interrupts my thought process.

"And by the way, there are seventy-two bars per box and nine boxes per row on the pallet. And you can use these calculators. Questions?"

*So . . . you are testing to see if we know how to use calculators?*

Everyone is clear, and we start. I grab a box of dark chocolate bars and put it on the pallet. Hmmmm. Seventy-two times nine times seven plus the box I put on. 4,608. I hand him the sheet seven seconds later.

"4,608. Perfect again. Nice work."

*No big deal. Learned basic multiplication in college when I got my accounting degree.*

The other person hands the sheet to him, and he checks it. His is perfect as well, but the third guy has screwed up the math. I see our test administrator dock him some points. Ouch. The two of us who got it right have risen a bit above the pack. He then says we can go to the office to see Natalia.

Natalia tells the other two guys to go see Lisa, and tells me to go with her.

"We're going to have you do a typing test. The directions are on the computer. Come find me when you are done."

I think she is able to see, despite the oversized fleece I am wearing, that there is no way I will be able to carry fifty-pound boxes of chocolate all day long. I probably wouldn't last an hour before breaking my back, thus the office test. I sit down at a desk with shit everywhere. Just like the whole factory, the office is extremely cluttered, and people are rushing around with paper and boxes of chocolate. I am still a little blurry-eyed from the beers I had last night and the sleep I didn't get.

Number one. Open up Internet Explorer. I imagine people getting up and saying they don't know how to do number one, and promptly getting thrown out. Number two. Go to this website. Done. Number three. Pick this test and start typing while trying to limit the amount of mistakes. I begin and am a little rusty. I keep screwing up and have to backspace but keep my cool and quickly the minute is up. Sixty-nine words a minute, with one mistake. Not bad. Natalia comes over to record my score on my sheet.

I am ready for more tests. I want to test my strength or my ability to navigate rows and rows of fancy chocolate. I want to be given hypothetical situations with the clock ticking and millions of dollars on the line, but it looks like the hour-long job fair will end in ten minutes—less time than we spent waiting in the lobby downstairs. I sit down at a desk, and Natalia asks me the final questions.

"When can you start?"

"Anytime."

"You ever worked in a warehouse before?"

"Many times."

"You ever driven a forklift or pallet jack?"

"Yes." *Don't insult me. Of course I have.*

"What shifts could you work?"

"All of them. Back to back if necessary."

"All right, that's it. Thanks for coming."

I head back to the maze and can't remember how to get out. I go through a door, down some stairs, and end up behind the building, near the Chicago River. It looks like a good place to get mugged, so I quickly shuffle around the corner to get back to the street where my car is parked.

I never do hear back from the factory. I guess in these desperate economic times, sixty-nine words a minute with one mistake just doesn't cut it.

# FOOD STAMP NATION

"Do you consider your neighborhood very safe, somewhat safe, or very unsafe?"

"Oh, well, I like people."

"Okay, ma'am, I understand. But would you consider your neighborhood very safe, somewhat safe, or very unsafe?"

"I like walking."

"Hmmm, okay, ma'am, that's good. But for this question, I need to put down one of these responses, so let me know which answer is best. Very safe. Somewhat safe. Very unsafe."

"I like my neighborhood."

"Okay, and that's fine, but I *need* you to choose one of the required answers, or I will get in trouble. Please pick one of these three words. *Very* safe, *somewhat* safe, or very *unsafe*."

"Oh, it's safe."

"Okay, great, ma'am. Very safe or somewhat safe?"

"It's usually safe."

"Ma'am, choose one of the following words as the next word that comes out of your mouth. VERY or SOMEWHAT."

My head is about to explode.

It was 4:40 p.m., and I had twenty minutes to go before getting off for holiday break. Then someone picked up, which was ideal, as these surveys last about twenty minutes, so theoretically it would take me right to the end of the day. Not so fast. The respondent turns out to be a senile woman who is both hard of hearing and *refuses* to give me answers I can use. I had improved the situation a few minutes ago when I realized that, besides giving me terrible answers, she is nearly deaf.

"Where do you shop for groceries?"

"My nephew visits me on the holidays."

"Ma'am, where do you shop for food!"

"God gives me the strength to make it through each day."

"Ma'am, I am going to call you back. We are having some technical difficulties."

I go over to the boss and ask where the special phone is for situations like this. He hands it to me, and I call the woman back. Basically, this phone amplifies my voice about five times. I ask her if the volume situation has improved, and she says that it has.

*Thank God.* Maybe we will get through this after all.

Unfortunately, the volume was only a small part of the disconnect between us. She doesn't understand that I have to choose a response from my screen. This response or that response. Yes or no. This number or that number. Questions that should take about five seconds each are taking an agonizing minute to answer.

"Ma'am, how often in the last thirty days did you feel that you weren't eating enough food because you just couldn't afford it? Very often, somewhat often, or never?"

"Oh, I love food."

"We all do, ma'am. We all do. But this question isn't actually asking about your feelings towards food. It's asking how often you weren't eating *enough* because you couldn't afford more food."

"God always provides."

My head pounds with frustration. "Ma'am. I am sitting in front of a computer, and I have a question on the screen, which I just read to you. There are three answers to this question that I can choose from. You have to tell me one of them, or we can't move on."

"Oh, okay. People help me out with food if I need it."

"That's great, ma'am, but for *this* question, which response works best for you? Very often, somewhat often, or never? Pick one of those three. Any one of those three."

"My nephew takes me to the store sometimes."

Do I hang up now, scream at her, repeat the question again, or choose for her and get in trouble for tampering with the survey? I put "I don't know," and move on.

———————

This is the second survey I am working on for a public policy company. The first dealt with all of the substance abuse treatment facilities in the country. This one deals with the food stamp program, which is now known as SNAP (Supplemental Nutrition Assistance Program). For some reason, none of the recipients we are calling seem to know that it is called SNAP and are constantly confused when questions refer to SNAP.

"Whoa, whoa, whoa. What is SNAP? I ain't on no SNAP! You talkin' all crazy!"

"Sir, as mentioned in the introduction to this survey, SNAP is the new name of the food stamp program. It was changed a few years ago. When I say SNAP, I am referring to food stamps."

"Oh, okay."

———————

Due to the Recession and the general trend of wealth distribution in the country, the amount of people on the program is at an all-time high—upwards of forty-six million people in a country with a population of three-hundred-eight million. This is supposed to be the wealthiest country in the world. Yet, every day, I talk to people who haven't graduated from high school and have had three kids by the time they are nineteen. I talk to people who don't know the definition of balanced. I talk to people in states where I cannot understand *anything* they are saying—and they are speaking English. I talk to people who don't have any way to cook their food. I talk to homeless people we happen to catch in a shelter. It is an eye-opening survey and one that is supposed to have an impact. It is designed to see how well SNAP is working and whether families are getting enough to eat. I just read an article about how thousands of people across the country gather at Walmarts around 11:30 p.m. on the last day of the month. This is because many of the SNAP benefits get reloaded at the beginning of the month; people want to check out right at midnight because they literally ran out of food days earlier.

We had run out of numbers to call a couple days ago, so all of the interviewers hung out and talked about surveys we had done. We joked about interviewing each other because most of us should be on food stamps ourselves. We offer gift cards to people who complete the survey, which is the main reason people participate, because it does take 15–20 minutes to finish. All of us interviewers would gladly take this incentive.

---

There is a lot of downtime when you are trying to contact people, so it gives me an opportunity to listen to others. I write down my favorite characteristics of my coworkers. The introduction of our survey says that we are doing it for the US Department of Agriculture, which is the branch of the government that funds SNAP.

One guy always says, "Ma'am, I'm calling from the United States Department of Agriculture," as if that sounds more legitimate than saying US.

Then there is my favorite guy from the last survey who speaks about ten words a minute. "Ma'am, I understand. That. Your. Time. Is Very. Valuable. But I must. Read. Every. Question. As. Worded. So that. Everyone. Hears the same. Survey. Thank you." Despite that, people never hang up on him. Casey Kasem couldn't perform any better.

There is one girl from Puerto Rico who could easily work as a voice actress for a children's fantasy movie or cartoon. Her voice is high with incredible inflection, and I love listening to her do surveys.

The guy with his MBA from Northwestern is back on board for this one. "Hello. My name is John . . . Studabaker. And I'm calling . . ." That pause before his last name is golden.

Another guy from the previous survey is back as well. Instead of saying, "My name is," he says, "Hi, it's Mike from the US . . . " As if to say, "Yeah, you know me, Mike, from the US Department of Agriculture? You don't remember me? We've had so many pleasant phone interviews in the past."

One girl who takes the job very seriously repeats the respondent's name in every sentence. "Well, Mel, I'm going to be asking you some important questions. Is that okay, Mel? How many people live in your household, Mel? You said four, Mel? Oh, five? Okay, Mel. Thank you." I counted during one survey, and she used that person's name over fifty times in less than twenty minutes.

The guy who sits next to me, and moved here from New York City by way of Brazil, says, "Thank you very much," after every response people give. "You're twenty years old? Thank you very much, sir. Now, when did you last shop for food? Last week? Thank you very much for that. Now . . . "

---

The survey itself gives me plenty to think about. We deal with people who are in desperate situations, and we have to remain professional throughout the survey. One person says she just got fired because she broke her leg and wasn't able to get to work. That same person, when asked how much help she would get from family living nearby, said none, even though her son lives three houses down. Many people don't eat for several days throughout the month because they have no money for food. Surprisingly, a lot of these people are upbeat and hopeful for the future. There is a section of the survey that asks about their feelings, and most people don't feel hopeless or think that things are a lost cause. This is unexpected, since a lot of them talk about how they never get enough food to eat.

Of course, there are some that aren't too keen to talk to us and seem to have a more negative outlook. I get to one voicemail system. "Yeah, this is Darren. Go ahead and leave me a message and I *might* return your call . . . but . . . I probably won't. If you *really* feel like you need to or you *really* want to, then go ahead and do it if it makes you feel better. Make. It. Happen. I just won't call you back."

Who has a voicemail message like this?

At least this guy gave an indication of who he is. Most people say nothing at all, or they say something like, "You know who it is. Hit me back." I have to check a box after each call that asks if the voicemail indicated the correct respondent; ninety-nine percent of the time I don't check it.

———————

Finally, I am in the last section with the senile woman. *Lord, this lady said you always provide, so guide me through this. Let this end, so that I may leave this building.*

My prayer is answered when the woman manages to give coherent and logical responses the rest of the time. The survey ends up taking forty-five minutes, which is three times longer than my average, but it does allow me plenty of time to regain a sense of urgency for the job hunt. This position is only going for a few more weeks. If my coworkers and I don't find real jobs soon, we might be headed to the SNAP office ourselves.

# THE FATS AND THE CURIOUS

"Y'all are a looongggg way from home."

I want to tell this guy that we are actually only a two-hour flight from home, but as he is wearing a bloodstained apron and holding a huge carving knife, I choose to agree with his statement.

"Yeah. Yeah, we are, but it's good to be in Nashville, Georgia. Nice town."

"Y'all don't like that Obama guy, do ya?"

"Ha ha. No, of course not. We just live in Chicago. Go Romney. Hey Krisztina, I'm going to do the street segment."

I quickly exit.

What the hell am I doing here? Earlier today, I walked by numerous Confederate flags and a monument to their former president, Jefferson Davis.

I had been excited when I learned I was going to Nashville, until I saw that it was not the Tennessee version, but rather a town of 5,000 in southern Georgia, 200 miles south of Atlanta.

I have heard the phrase, "Y'all ain't from around here," no less than ten times—maybe more, but I can't understand much of the local dialect. I could understand Russian better than some of the English I have heard around these parts.

I walk along a trash-strewn road outside the butcher shop and pick up about ten cigarette packs, placing them in small plastic bags. Eventually, my partner, Krisztina, makes it out of the store alive, and we head back to the car. We drive a few blocks to do some more street segments and come to an area that looks like it has been ravaged by a tornado. There are unoccupied trailer homes distributed throughout the block, a school bus turned over on its side covered with graffiti, and piles of yard debris everywhere. I slow down to take a picture of a sign that says "No Trust-passing," when suddenly I see a menacing-looking man walking quickly towards me. I hastily pull onto a different street and head towards our next observation.

---

A few weeks ago, when asked by a girl at a bar in Chicago what I did for a living, I replied, "I travel around the country looking for fat kids."

I was only half joking. In February, I applied for a position at a local university that is conducting an adolescent obesity study. Due to the recent spike in child diabetes rates and widespread interest on the subject, one of the country's largest health-related philanthropic foundations funded a study to find the cause of the obesity problem and, ultimately, what could be done to mitigate it.

Different arguments can be made for why the problem exists—be it subsidized corn turned into high fructose corn syrup that is subsequently put into all of our food, kids' sedentary lifestyles with the advent of video games and non-stop TV entertainment, or a combination of these and other reasons. The point is, more kids have diabetes than ever before, and it is driving up health care costs significantly. I read that the current generation of youths may be the first in American history to have a lower life expectancy than their parents.

This summer is the third year of data collection. They needed thirty-two research specialists to travel to over 160 sites throughout the country to spend the summer filling out a variety of forms to be analyzed by policy experts and statistics gurus. They wanted people who were comfortable traveling, knew how to navigate and drive through different cities, and would be able to efficiently code data, since we would only be in these sites for a week at a time. My experience traveling the country to play ultimate, as well as my Census and public policy telephone interviewing jobs, contributed to qualifying me for the gig. That, and my disdain for fat kids.

———————

I show up for training in a room full of thirty-one strangers. We each receive a gigantic binder covering every aspect of the project in excruciating detail. Essentially, we will be filling out a series of forms. We will walk up and down streets, visit parks, school grounds, physical activity venues, food stores, tobacco shops, and fast food restaurants. Each form has upwards of one hundred boxes to fill out—for example, on the food form, we look for the availability of certain items, and record prices. On the street segment form, we look at land uses, whether there are pedestrian crossing points, bike lanes, parking lots, street lighting, and dozens of other factors. At schools and parks, we look for sports features. At restaurants, we examine the availability of certain menu items, record prices, and look for health information. We also pick up cigarette packs to look at taxes in different parts of the country. Another university will interview students in all of the communities we visit, in order to analyze their health over time. Our data will be combined with their results, and somehow, when it is all said and done, the millions of checkmarks we record will amount to some revelation about what factors contribute to obesity.

When I explain this to a friend, he is incredulous. "Aren't kids fat because they are lazy and eat shitty food?"

Point taken—but don't kill the messenger. In training, we learned how a lot of things seem obvious in hindsight. We were told that studies like these provided the evidence to ban smoking in hospitals, airplanes, and other places that seem unimaginable to smoke in these days. They told us that some people still don't believe in climate change, so these studies are vital to sway public opinion and to help provide concrete evidence to policy makers.

I don't really care either way, nor do most of the people on this job. We are taking it because we get to travel the country on the University's dime. The trainers show us a map of the 160 sites we will visit. We are going to forty-three of the lower forty-eight states. Apparently, there are no obese kids in Nebraska, the Dakotas, Utah, or Montana.

———————

After three weeks of learning the forms, taking numerous quizzes, and doing a bunch of team-building exercises involving Hula-Hoops, we are ready for our mock catchment. We go with a partner to a community in the Greater Chicagoland area for two days to practice coding. I am paired with a woman from the South Side, and we meet in Maywood, which is a moderately sketchy suburb just west of the city. We go into a convenience store, and I begin coding the food store form. Moments later, the proprietor is right in front of me.

"What are you doing!"

"Oh, hello, sir. We are doing a school project, looking at food and tobacco availability in the area."

"I don't know what you do. You just come in here and start writing things? I don't know where you come from. If you just talk to me, then I let you do project!"

He is not happy with me, but that is why we practice. From now on, in the real sites, I always talk to small shop owners to avoid awkward confrontations. Out in the field, we have an official letter from the dean of the university that briefly explains the project. It states that we are not stealing information, are not competitors, and that no information will ever be shared, just aggregated with hundreds of other stores' information. This usually placates paranoid shopkeepers, but we do get kicked out every so often. In Whittier, California, a man accused me of stealing.

"You get out now. You steal from my store! You get out!"

"Actually, sir . . . "

"Get out!"

"Peace." I scram.

In these instances, you don't want to be confrontational—just get the hell out of there. The shitty part is that we need to replace these stores by going to another similar establishment. In a recent meeting after a few weeks out in the field, everyone related stories of crazy workers they had come across. One girl was nearly assaulted as the man snatched her forms from her. She retaliated by saying she would call the cops, and he eventually returned them. He then watched her like a hawk until she left the parking lot.

These instances are few and far between. Most people are interested in the project and are glad to help.

In the same meeting, we spent about an hour hearing about other hairy situations from the field. One guy was reluctant to tell his story again, but was coaxed into it by those that had not heard it. He was in rural Texas, and a man drove up next to him and verbally abused him with sexually explicit language, asking him to get in his truck so that they could "have a good time." My coworker said he was cornered on a dead-end road doing the street segment. There were fields on both sides and a lake at the other, and he didn't know how to swim. He was still shaken up a couple weeks after.

Another team was locked in a school parking lot and had to call the cops to have it opened up for them. One team inadvertently went to a high-security prison that was mistakenly labeled as a local school. One guy, when picking up cigarettes, didn't realize there was a snake in one of the packs, and when he got back to the car, the snake fell in and started slithering around. That same guy got his car broken into a few days later in Hollywood, Florida, and all of his stuff was stolen.

There was one totaled car, another with significant damage, numerous flat tires, and a busted radiator. One team in Birmingham, Alabama said they heard gunshots and reported that there were numerous prostitutes in their hotel. My most exciting story to share with the group was when Krisztina and I went kayaking in Okefenokee Swamp during the Nashville trip. With no one else around, it was eerily silent and pretty frightening to be kayaking next to hundreds of alligators. At one point, on our way back in, one alligator slammed into the bottom of her kayak, and she let out a shriek as she rocked back and forth. We believe it just didn't see the kayak, and disaster, once again, was averted. I didn't think the alligators were a big deal until moments after returning the kayak, I saw one of them crush a large turtle in its jaws like it was eating a potato chip. I saw the legs and neck of the turtle squirming until the alligator finished the job. I was glad I didn't see this National Geographic moment before our outing.

---

The most interesting part of the gig was exploring areas all over the US I would never otherwise go, and meeting some really memorable characters.

In Nashville, Georgia, we had been coding the butcher because it was on our list of primary grocery stores. The guy said he could clean and chop up anything—people had brought in deer, bears, raccoons, and an assortment of other woodland creatures. I felt like I had entered a scene in *Deliverance*, so I bailed.

My first week was in Wetumpka, Alabama—about as Deep South as you can get, and it had a similar vibe to Nashville. This is where the movie *Big Fish* was filmed, and I felt like I had gone back in time a few decades. Every time we mentioned we came from Chicago, people were amazed.

"Ooooh. Y'all from the North. Y'all have come a long way for this." The south fits the stereotype—life moves very slowly down there, but people are extremely friendly. Unfortunately, vegetarian fare was not easy to find, and I was forced to consume quite a bit of barbeque during my stay.

Week two catapulted us towards the other end of the socioeconomic spectrum. Whittier, California—a Los Angeles suburb. Instead of mobile homes and roads that wouldn't be out of place in a horror movie, there were bike lanes, vegan restaurants, and nutritional information on menus. I took the opportunity to visit friends in Hollywood and practice my Spanish when coding fast food taquerías.

Week three was in Chiefland, Florida—back to the South. This involved a flight to Tampa, and then a two-hour drive to the site. Like Alabama, cigarettes were super cheap, and every gas station had about thirty signs advertising different kinds of tobacco.

In week six, we went to Liberty, South Carolina. All I remember from that trip was seeing woodchucks everywhere, stumbling upon dozens of black widow spiders near our hotel, and seeing the devastation of the Great Recession. The main street was eighty percent vacant and littered with boarded-up businesses. We talked to an older couple who ran the local hot dog restaurant that we coded, and they said things had been pretty tough in recent years. Manufacturing and tobacco-related jobs had dried up, so there just wasn't much economic activity in the area.

One of the highlights was week five in Crescent City, California. This town has the distinction of being the most tsunami-prone place in the continental United States. In fact, one person died here from the tsunami that hit Japan in 2011. The town has been destroyed more than once, but it keeps getting rebuilt due to the rich fishing waters. Instead of ninety-degree heat like the rest of the sites, it was in the fifties and drizzling the entire time. This was also the area where part of *Return of the Jedi* was filmed—the Ewok scenes.

We met some botanists from the University of California-Berkeley at dinner one night. They told us that in their biased opinion, this particular part of California was the most beautiful area in the world. That convinced us to visit numerous redwood groves, and after a few hikes among 1000-year-old trees and bright green foliage, I was close to agreeing.

———

I was still working, filling out forms, but in reality, it had taken a backseat to exploring the sites. Everyone spent time planning things to do and restaurants to visit. I went from rural places to cities after the Crescent City trip. I went to Williamston, Michigan; Kansas City, Missouri; a small Pennsylvania town in the heart of Amish country; Brooklyn, New York; Satellite Beach, Florida; and finally, Scio, New York.

Williamston was the exact opposite of all the southern towns I visited. There were signs on every street, a plethora of parks, and numerous swanky restaurants downtown. It seemed hard to believe I was just an hour from Detroit.

I took a duck boat tour in Philly, despite the infamous incident a couple years back when a barge pulverized the tour boat, killing two Romanian students. Our tour went off without any issues, and I learned a lot of United States history.

In Brooklyn, I was puzzled as to why residents couldn't put garbage in garbage cans, and seemed content wading through piles of trash. The rats were impressive, as were the train delays.

I learned that Kansas City is one of the top disc golf cities in the country and that Lancaster County is the epicenter of the Amish in the United States. I nearly ran my car into the back of a dozen horse buggies in the countryside. Standing in line waiting for ice cream next to some Amish kids, I couldn't understand a word of the Pennsylvania Dutch they were speaking.

---

The other aspect of the job was getting to know the random thirty-one others with whom I trained months earlier. Each week, I worked with one partner, and often times, would be in a multi-team site. There was one common link among us: none of us could procure a permanent position. Most were in their twenties and had graduated college, but weren't sure what to do. Everyone would ask each other what they were doing after the season ended, and the response was always, "Not sure."

I worked directly with seven people—all women. One partner had been laid off at a major consulting firm, and came across this job. She will best be remembered for nearly breaking my neck every time she hit the brakes and her extreme fear of animals. The only way I could describe her reaction to seeing a small dog is that it would be similar to the look of ter-ror a parent would have if seeing her child get mauled by a bear.

Another of my partners didn't eat—ever. If she did, it had to be frozen yogurt. Krisztina, my partner with the alligator incident, was from Hungary. She was always down to do anything adventurous, even if it meant walking by black widows or paddling with alligators. Another of my partners was Mexican, and I spent time practicing Spanish with her. One woman was living in Chicago just for the summer but went to graduate school in Portland. My second to last partner was giving up on Chicago as well, in order to return home to Detroit to look for work.

My last partner was a woman in her sixties who really enjoyed this position. When we convinced her to come out with us in Kansas City after telling her we would be back by ten, she said, "I've heard that a million times. I know how you kids are these days. First it's 10:00, then 11:00, and then all of a sudden, it's 3:00 in the morning." Still, she came and actually enjoyed herself, saying she was really impressed with Kansas City.

A common joke we made when returning to the airport each Friday was, "This has been a good vacation . . . I mean work week." I can't imagine there being many jobs like this one. In Satellite Beach, Florida, my partner and I spent more than twelve hours trying to find manatees because we had finished our work early.

———————

In the past, one of my security questions for an online bank asked what my dream job was, and my response was to be an explorer. This job truly fit the bill. I drove thousands of miles through a dozen states visiting stores, parks, schools, and restaurants. I talked to hundreds of random people from different walks of life. I saw some extremely beautiful areas as well as some disturbing sites I never want to see again. Sometimes, I get frustrated with this country, with its anemic political system and economic disparity, but this job reminded me why it is such a great place, with its diverse geography and culture. Depressingly, I don't know how the gig will help me in the future, but hopefully down the road, if kids start getting healthier, you'll know one person to thank.

# NO EXTRA CREDIT

I know Chicago pretty well, but I have never been to this part of town. I am on the southwest side of the city looking for a nondescript warehouse that serves as headquarters for a TV show called *Chicago Fire.* There are no addresses anywhere but I eventually guess correctly. There is a woman at a desk in an otherwise empty front room.

"Hello. My name is Andrew Edwards. I'm here for the costume fitting."

"You're early."

"Really? I thought they said 2:30."

"You'll just have to wait for a while."

I am escorted to a back room with fairly regular foot traffic. In front of me are hundreds of costumes that will be used for an upcoming scene in one of the early episodes. I am to be an extra in a Halloween block party scene. They had asked for people to bring in their own costumes, so I brought my Mario costume from another gig. They want to inspect all of the extras in their costumes ahead of time.

After reading for several minutes, a woman pops in and says she is ready for me. I tell her that I have a Mario costume, but she says they can't use it because of copyright infringement. They have plenty of other costumes I can use, and since I am the very first person here, I get first pick. I choose a Duff Beer Man costume, a popular character from *The Simpsons.* It takes thirty seconds to put on and then a couple of staffers look me up and down.

"Deb, you'll need to cover that Duff Beer stuff and tighten the waist a few inches. Other than that, he should be good."

Someone else takes a picture of me and tells me to change back into my clothes. I sign some agreement without reading it, and leave.

———————

Two weeks later it is time for the shoot. I have no idea what to expect since this is my first foray into the entertainment industry. I bring a magazine to read and not much else because we were told that there is nowhere to store personal belongings.

The meeting place is a church on the North Side in the Lincoln Park neighborhood. There is already a long queue out the door stretching down the block, as there will be nearly 150 extras needed tonight. Slowly but surely, I advance in the line and make my way to the basement to sign the requisite papers. I go to the back where the costumes are stored and receive my tailored Duff Beer Man costume. Thirty seconds later, I'm suited up and ready for action.

The basement is not big enough for the situation at hand. Several tables have been roped off and are reserved for staff and actors only. The extras are herded into the corner, awkwardly crammed into tiny chairs that do not quite accommodate our costumes.

The crowd resembles a real Halloween party. People are walking all over the place in incredibly elaborate getups. This is a big-budget show and it isn't skimping on costs. Since they can't have any copyrighted characters, everyone is dressed up in generic outfits. I see several monsters, butterflies, goblins, construction workers, mad scientists, zombies, ghosts, doctors, and dozens of others. The vast majority of the female costumes are incredibly slutty. The producers know that sex sells and have picked the most revealing costumes imaginable—sexy nurses, sexy vampires, sexy pumpkins, sexy anything. I have been to strip clubs with dancers that revealed less than these women.

Eventually, one of the set managers comes out and yells that he needs the restaurant scene people. Fifteen extras leave while the rest of us remain in the cramped basement. I read a few articles in my magazine, and before I know it, an hour has passed and I have done absolutely nothing. The same guy who called away the restaurant scene extras returns and announces that there is food outside. Over one hundred people jump up and make a dash for the stairs to check out the catering. Several passersby do double takes as our crew emerges from the bowels of the church, still clad in our costumes. After filling up our plates with subpar-looking pasta, bread, and fruit, we head back in to eat and continue waiting. I turn to a person sitting next to me.

"Do you know the schedule of the shoot or anything for that matter?"

"Nope."

I read a few more articles in *Wired*, but am starting to get antsy. I only brought one magazine with me and didn't expect this much down time. Three hours have passed since I arrived and none of us have moved with the exception of our trip to the buffet.

The manager shows up again and says that he needs the mad scientist for his scene. A guy dressed up as a mad scientist with blood all over his face shuffles by.

That could have been me.

I received a call a week ago asking me to try out for a featured extra role. It was to be part of an important plot point—a party attendee dressed as a mad scientist will have a seizure in middle of the party, which is when the paramedics show up. The director really liked my image and wanted to meet me to see if I would be a good fit. I originally said yes, but then reneged a couple days later and emailed them that I didn't really want to do it after all. A few things had come up and I didn't want to drive back down to the studio to audition for a non-paid role that wasn't a guarantee.

Apparently, the email never got to them because they called me several days later to verify my meeting with the director. When I told them I had sent an email, they were pissed.

"You can't just back out of a featured extra role."

"Sorry," I had said. "I emailed you guys and thought it was taken care of."

They asked me why I didn't want to do it and I replied that it just wasn't my scene, pun certainly intended.

If I had gotten the gig, that would be me leaving now to learn my part, but it isn't, and I remain with the rest of the extras.

After forty-five more minutes, we finally get word that we are about to move. We march upstairs and wait outside the church, then another call is given and we head out. It is nighttime now, and the temperature has dropped into the seventies, which is a lot more comfortable than the stuffy basement. We walk a few blocks, turn a corner, and the shining lights of the set are ahead of us.

It is an elaborate setup along a street lined with bars and restaurants all decked out with cheesy Halloween decorations. There is equipment and lights poking out from every direction, and there are staff members running around putting on finishing touches. There is a DJ stage up front, and lots of local residents hanging out, watching everything unfold.

The extras trickle into place.

The scene will be simple. We are at a street costume party, dancing and having a good time. Then the mad scientist will do his thing, the medics will come and do their thing, and then it will be over. Couldn't be easier.

What I am about to discover, though, is that each scene will be done a million times, from a million angles, and there will be several minutes between each take.

We get ready for the first take.

A guy yells, "Rolling!" Numerous others echo his call.

A few seconds later, he yells "Action!"

The DJ up on stage starts spinning some dance music. Everyone begins to dance and we all pretend to talk to each other. We are told to be quiet, as the sound will be edited later. After a few seconds, the music is cut, and everyone continues to dance to the same rhythm, still pretending to talk. It is very unusual seeing a hundred people dance without music, but apparently this is the norm.

After about fifteen seconds, someone else yells, "Cut!" and we stop moving. For the next five minutes we hang out in small groups talking and waiting for our next order.

The music starts again and suddenly the elevated train zooms by just fifty feet from us and the director cancels the take. This will happen over a dozen times throughout the night. I want to tell them that I have an app on my phone that will tell me exactly when trains come by here, but I don't actually care. In fact, the longer we are here, the better it is for us, since we get paid time and a half after eight hours.

We spend an hour shooting a thirty-second scene.

Finally, it is time for the mad scientist segment. I glance over curiously to see what this role would have required of me. He is lying on his back and convulsing violently, then two paramedics scream at people to get out of the way, and put him on the stretcher. This scene is reshot at least ten times.

Another guy, who seems to be in charge, comes up to our group and picks out a few people, including me. He tells us to go to the other side of the street where the ambulance truck is located. We will be there to get pushed out of the way for the close up shots of when the firefighters get here. I face Catwoman and we bounce and sway to the imaginary music for a few moments, and then several of the actual cast in their firefighter getups barge through.

"Excuse me! Get out of the way! Excuse me."

We act surprised as they storm by us. After thirty seconds, everyone resets, waits five minutes, and we go again for another take.

The next scene is when the mad scientist gets loaded into the ambulance. After watching a few takes, I don't regret my decision to turn down the position, even if it means I am not guaranteed to be on TV. The guy looks worn out after doing the same seizure action two dozen times.

It has now been eight hours since we got here and we are told that pizza has arrived. Everyone breaks and scrambles to a table where thirty large pizzas are laid out. I hand out plates and the slices disappear faster than free bags of rice in Mogadishu.

Are we done? Apparently not.

We now have to do everything over again so that the scenes can be shot from the other angle. I am dismayed. We may not get out of here until five in the morning. I am fine getting some overtime, but did not plan on watching the sunrise.

For the new scenes, I am placed in front again, but this time I am situated at a table, pretending to grab a beer from a keg. For each take, I do the same thing, putting my hand up to indicate that I want a beer.

Then we move on to the seizure scene again. I look around and people are definitely beginning to zone out. Some people sit down between takes and others lean against buildings. This was fun at first, but now our knees and feet hurt from standing, and we want it to be over.

In the meantime, the director has several people walk back and forth on the sidewalk, doing a loop. Others do the same dance moves on repeat. I am taken across the street to be one of the people coming to the party for an alternate angle of a scene we shot earlier. After the scene begins, an assistant director describes my sequence to me. I am to remain slightly behind the goblin in front of me and go in a different entrance to the party. I casually walk across the street and people give me high fives as I enter. Then I return to my spot and do it again. I do this at least eight times but then am told that they won't be using this part after all. That could have been my only chance at actually being seen in the episode.

I have discovered that I am one of the few randoms to take part in this shoot; most people here are somehow tied to the entertainment industry. Many are actors, writers, or production people. Earlier in the evening, I heard people complaining about some extras that didn't know what they were doing (like me) and slowing things down. I did not get involved with that conversation.

I spend the last thirty minutes hanging with a dude from Louisville who recently moved to Chicago to try to snag some acting roles. He has the best costume by far. It is a pinstripe zoot suit that has really wide shoulders and a crazy mask that makes him look like Frankenstein's monster. Someone thinks he is the bad guy from *Dick Tracy*. Despite the fact that we are nearly ten hours into the shoot, he is still dancing with an unparalleled ferocity. He has incredible moves and everyone encircles him during the shoots. Most people just bob back and forth, but this guy must really want to get on camera.

Finally, someone yells out over the megaphone that we are good to go. There is a stampede down the block as everyone returns to the church to change out of our costumes. I soon realize why there was a rush. We have to stand in line to get our paperwork finished so that we can get paid. Everyone is tired and wants to leave, but it still takes about a minute to handle each person. Thirty minutes pass before I get to the table. I sign the sheet and am free to leave. I end up getting home at three in the morning and immediately crash.

This will probably be my last acting role. For a person that hates waiting more than anything, this would be my job in hell. I just spent ten hours hanging out for a segment that will last three minutes in the actual show. Nope, not my scene at all.

# SPY DON'T KNOW ABOUT THIS

"Is this legal?" I ask.

There is a slight pause before Lewis my interviewer, responds, "Yeah, I think so. I wouldn't worry about it."

"Okay."

"So are you interested?"

"I suppose."

"Great. I will get you the paperwork later today. You can start training on Monday with Greg."

I leave the building wondering what I have just gotten myself into. I have worked a few sketchy jobs in the past, but this one has the potential to trump them all.

I will be performing research for a real estate company, finding out the identity of the office tenants in virtually every building in the downtown business district of Chicago. In order to do this, I will bypass security by whatever method I can manage, and go floor-by-floor documenting the building's occupants—a process called "stacking."

The easy part is typing in company names and suite numbers. The hard part, as explained by Lewis, is getting into the buildings in the first place. Chicago has some of the tallest and most modern office skyscrapers in the world. This means that many of them have security desks, cameras all over the place, and turnstiles requiring key cards.

This isn't going to be easy.

I had never heard of such a job before and didn't apply for this one. My friend Erin, who I worked with on a university adolescent obesity study[10], had stumbled onto this gig a few weeks earlier. During her interview, she recounted her experience recording data covertly in stores all over the country for the obesity study. Lewis asked her if she was the type to seal the deal or to score digits by the end of the night—essentially, was she someone that could make things happen. The "stacker," as this position is called, would have to be a smooth talker and be able to slip through doors unnoticed. And the information would need to be gathered quickly and discreetly. Erin said the right things and got the gig. Her assigned partner bailed the day before she was scheduled to start, so Lewis asked Erin if she knew anyone that would be a good fit for the position, and more importantly, a person who could start soon. I was interviewed the next day.

---

The paperwork is dense, so I am unable to start right away. The office guy, Greg, who recommended the flake that bailed, has to work the streets with Erin for several days until I can officially begin.

When I finally show up for my first day, the training method employed is trial by fire. I meet Greg outside a modern office building in the financial district. He tells me that the first step is to do outside reconnaissance. We circle the building looking for different entrances, and in this particular case, there is just one entrance. We then glance into the large lobby, where there is a security desk with two guards and two elevator banks—one set for floors 2–15 and the other for floors 16–30. We watch a few workers go in and notice that they have to click a keycard at the security desk before going to the elevators. This is what is defined as a medium-security building. There are guards and a keycard, but no turnstiles, which would make it a high-security building. In this building, we can try to sneak by the desk and go straight for the elevators.

Greg goes in first, heads to the elevators, and is immediately stopped. He begins to talk with one of the guards. I come in a few seconds later,

---

10  See "The Fats and the Curious"

glance at my phone, and walk to the other set of elevators like it's no big deal. I, too, get stopped because I don't have a keycard with me.

"Sir, you need to check in."

"Okay. Sorry about that."

"Who are you here to see?"

Before entering, Greg and I each looked over an outdated program on an iPad that lists some of the known tenants in each of the buildings. I picked out a financial services company that looked promising.

"Venus Capital."

"Very good. And who are you seeing today?"

The only name listed in the program was the CEO of the company.

"John Roberts."

"Okay. Here is a temporary keycard. Take the left elevators to the eighteenth floor."

"Thank you."

I turn and head to the elevators. I quickly glance over to see that Greg has been denied. His story doesn't check out. I overhear him mumble about having the wrong building before shuffling out. I am now on my own.

I ride up to the thirtieth floor, and get to work. As I leave the elevator, I glance down at my phone to look preoccupied. With these modern office buildings, many of the floors are occupied by only a couple of tenants, so employees recognize new faces. Thus, it is imperative that I work quickly to avoid suspicion. On floors with multiple tenants, I have the advantage of people thinking that I have an appointment with some other company on the same floor.

I do five floors in just a few minutes. I walk around, typing on my phone like I am waiting for an appointment. I am wearing business casual clothes and am clean-shaven, so I fit in just fine. All I do is look at the directories or signs on doors and record the tenants and suite numbers on my phone. Then, I move to the next floor.

It gets awkward when I arrive on a floor that houses a single company with a desk right outside the elevators. This happens about ten floors in. I begin to step out of the elevator and see that there is a woman sitting at the reception desk of a major law firm.

"Hello. Can I help you?"

I glance around like I'm trying to find a sign for the company, and make a face of concern.

"Is this Avatar Consulting?"

"No, this is Smith and Roebuck Law Firm."

"Damn. Wrong floor. Sorry."

"It's okay," she says with a smile, and I get back into the elevator recording Smith and Roebuck into my phone.

After forty-five minutes, I descend, quickly walk by security, exit the building, and meet Greg, who is with Erin at a designated coffee shop.

"Nice work, rookie," he says.

"What can I say? I'm a natural."

While I was inside, they took interior and exterior pictures of the building. I send the completed stack to the data entry people in the office and look at the list to find the next building. The rest of the day goes by without a hitch, and the next day I will go at it alone, and Greg can return to his regular desk job.

At a meeting a couple days later, Erin and I meet Lewis to go over a few things. Although he has explained it before, I ask him once more about the purpose of this job.

"Why are we doing this? I still don't understand how this information is used."

After he explains it again, it still seems convoluted.

Basically, in the real estate industry, there are all sorts of players—the building owners, the tenants, the property managers, the leasing team, and the brokers. They all have different incentives, and information isn't always openly available. Brokers know about certain tenants and buildings and try to find good deals for their clients. It is all about relationships and making connections. There is no one place to look up vacancies and see which tenants are where, so our company is doing on-the-ground research to find out where there is space available and which tenants are in competitors' buildings. We are essentially providing information for brokers to steal other brokers' clients down the road.

Lewis explains it more clearly.

"The brokers. These guys make $150K, $200K a year. In the past they have done their own stacking, looking for tenant leads, but it isn't worth their time. If we can have a ground team—i.e., you guys—to stack for much cheaper, then it will save the company a lot of money."

"I see . . ."

"Your work is extremely important and the data you collect will end up in an application that will be used by these brokers."

As I leave the meeting, I regret even asking the question. But there's no time to worry about it—I have to go do some dirty work for some brokers whose time is much more valuable than mine.

---

The cool part of the job is seeing the interior of many buildings I have walked by hundreds of times. Generally, the most unique ones are the historic buildings that are national landmarks. These are also the ones that usually don't have any security, so we can walk straight to the elevators without any fuss. If there is a security person, we just give them our name and up we go.

But there is no shortage of less-than-ideal situations.

One day, I arrive at a modern skyscraper loaded with financial firms and law offices. It is the same scenario as the first building I did—multiple elevator banks and a security desk with a keycard sensor. I try my usual method of walking to the elevator like I belong there.

"Excuse me, sir."

I walk over. "Hello."

"You need to check in."

"Right. I have an appointment at Sidman Consulting."

"Your name?"

"Andrew Edwards."

"Yeah . . . I'm not seeing you on the list. I'll call up."

Not good.

"Yeah, Andrew Edwards is here for his appointment." She frowns and nods. "Okay. Yeah, let me ask him." She turns to me. "They don't have any appointment for you, sir."

"Interesting. Yeah, I don't remember who I talked to, but they said I could come in at this time."

*I need to get out of here.*

"He says he doesn't remember who he talked to but that they told him to come in."

This goes on for another minute but I can tell I am not getting in. Other people have come up to the desk to go to real appointments, so I quietly say that I'll call Sidman outside, and quickly exit.

This happens a fair amount. Several places ask for your name, give you a badge, and send you on your way. But many of these nicer buildings require you to be on a list. I will try all sorts of tactics, but most don't work.

"I am here for an interview."

"I am just stopping by to follow up with an application I sent."

A few times, I give a name of a person that no longer works for the company or is out of the country. I smile, say that I looked at my calendar wrong, and flee. Erin tries a tactic where she tells the guard that she has an interview the next day, but she gets nervous and likes to prepare by visiting the actual office the day before. Despite the creativity of this method, she is denied.

The scariest encounter happens at another towering office building. I do my usual reconnaissance. There are two doors—the main entrance, where there is a security desk with multiple guards, and one on the side with just one security guard standing near the elevators. It doesn't appear that any keycards are required, so I slip in the side door, and walk with several people to the elevator.

It is lunchtime and there are all sorts of workers going in and out of the building. I do about ten floors and then get to one that has no signs. I walk around and see that every door has a keycard sensor, but nothing else. I record question marks for this floor and go down to the next floor. I get out of the elevator, turn right, and see metal detectors, an American Flag, and an armed guard. It is a Homeland Security office.

*Uh oh.*

The man immediately jumps up. "Hey! What are you doing?"

"Oh, nothing. I'm on the wrong floor." I push the elevator button.

The guard jogs out to me and says, "Kind of like you were on the wrong floor right above us."

*Shit.* He's been watching me on security cameras.

"Yeah, I just can't seem to find what I'm looking . . ."

He interrupts me. "We're going down to security."

We enter the elevator and make the trip down with him glaring at me the entire time. He grabs my arm and drags me to the security desk where the head security guy is waiting with several people.

"This is the guy," the government agent says.

"What are you doing?" the boss asks.

There are six guards including the armed guy next to me. Do I lie and play dumb, or do I play it straight? I opt for the latter.

"Oh, just doing some research on vacancies in the area."

"Check his bag," the boss says to the Homeland guy.

I begin to open my bag and then he screams, "Drop it! Step back!" I accommodate this request.

He rifles through my bag and says it's clean. They take my ID and run it through the system.

"We need to know how you got in."

"I just walked in, to the elevators."

"Who did you walk by?"

"I can't remember. I wasn't paying attention."

"We need to know."

"Well, I really don't know . . . I don't want to get anyone in trouble."

"There's going to be a lot of trouble if you don't tell us!" he screams.

"I honestly don't know. I am just looking at vacancies in the office market—that's it."

There are dozens of people shuffling by looking at the spectacle. I would love to not be here right now.

"Okay. You step foot in here again without a legitimate purpose and we'll arrest you."

"Fair enough. Thanks."

I walk outside, turn a corner, and quickly make my way to a café, all the while wondering how close I was to being arrested. I email Lewis, saying I wouldn't mind not returning to this partially-stacked building. I replay the events in my head, wondering if I could have handled it any better. This job is all about thinking quickly and this incident discouraged me.

A few days earlier, I did a better job of getting out of a jam. I had stumbled into a non-descript building that I was pretty sure was a data center. There was a security guard at the desk and I told her I was visiting Teksys Corp., which was the only company that came up in a Google search. She said I didn't have to check in with her, but rather at the end of the hall with another security guard. I walked over and the guy asked if I was going up.

"Oh, no. Just hanging out waiting for a buddy for lunch."

"Sounds good."

I walked back to a stairwell right by the original security guard's desk and made my way upstairs. Like James Bond, I slunk along a wall and tried not to make a sound. I peered around a corner but all of the doors were unmarked and required keycards. I decided I should get out. I then heard the guards talking on their radios.

"Yeah, that guy didn't come in here."

"Really? He said he was here for Teksys and headed in that direction."

*Gotta get out of here . . .*

I went back to the stairwell and tip toed down. When I got to the bottom, both guards were waiting for me.

"What are you doing?"

"Well, I have to be honest with you. I made up that thing about going to see Teksys Corp. I just had to go to the bathroom really bad."

The first guard frowned and said, "I would have let you use the bathroom. You didn't have to be so sneaky about it."

"I apologize. Thanks a lot."

Before they could interrogate me further, I slipped out into the real world.

---

Later in the week, I am at a get together with some friends I haven't seen in a while.

"Edwards, what are you doing right now?"

"I'm a spy." I say this with a straight face and no hint of sarcasm.

This job is changing me, even when I am not stacking. Every building I go into, my eyes dart around and I spot the three, the four, or the dozen security cameras hidden in a variety of places. I look from a distance to see how people get into buildings and whether or not there are security guards.

If I am being watched as I finish up a building, I will put the phone to my ear and say, "Mike, you're outside? Damn. I thought you told me to go up to your office. Yeah, Panera is fine with me." I maintain the charade until I am gone.

When I am on the floors of a building, I am constantly checking reflections in glass doors or TV screens to look for people behind me. If I hear voices, I will slip around corners, bathrooms, or stairwells. I do a lot of talking to fictitious people and take gratuitous drinks from water fountains.

"Hi honey, yeah, I am still waiting for the appointment with him. They told me to hang out for a few minutes. Just grabbing a drink in the hallway."

I am a shadow, just a regular guy that no one notices. When I am taking pictures, I make it look like I am texting. When a security guard glances away for a second, I take a shot. I use my peripheral vision to scan a room, looking for anything out of the ordinary, so I can bounce if the need arises.

My friend and I go to see the latest Bond film, *Skyfall,* which completes a yearlong marathon of watching all the Bond movies in order. As I watch 007 confidently walk through train stations and glance through crowds, I feel a connection to him. We both slip in side doors to do our work, and just as quickly disappear out of another one.

The main difference is that I am not saving the world. Quite the opposite, in fact. I am helping rich brokers compete against other rich brokers. Stacking is not a novel concept. Lewis explained to us that every company does it to their competitors' buildings. He had said building managers would catch us in the act from time to time and toss us out. This does happen once or twice, but most of the time, if we get in, we finish the stack. Erin gets called a piranha during her first week. I get kicked out of one building after sitting near the directory for way too long.

"Sir, what are you doing?"

"Just some research."

"Well, go do some research out of my building."

Besides the Homeland incident, most of these situations are benign. In smaller buildings, many of the tenants know each other, so they sometimes contact security because they are concerned with a stranger lurking around. I get kicked out a couple times by guards saying non-employees shouldn't be in the building. I usually say I am waiting for a friend and don't want to wait outside or that I am at the wrong address. The skill of lying to strangers becomes second nature.

––––––––––––––

After a few weeks, we have visited all the buildings except for the several dozen with turnstiles, but Lewis says it is okay not to attempt these ones. The likelihood of getting in is not worth it because with these, we would have to stop at the desk to concoct a story. Erin and I are thankful for this. Talking to security personnel can be a thrill sometimes, but most of the time it is agonizing. It is often a lose-lose proposition. The vast majority of the time, we don't get in at all. In the event that we do get up with a fictitious reason, the guard tells the company that Andrew Edwards is on his way up. But in reality Andrew Edwards will never actually go anywhere but to the top floor to start stacking. This proves to be problematic when the company calls back down to tell security that no such person has made an appearance. This situation has sent me to the streets on at least two occasions.

We spend the final few days returning to all of the unfinished buildings that were either straight-up denials or ones with turnstiles. We have to take pictures of them even though we don't have the accompanying stacks. Then there is a final meeting to review things.

"Incredible work guys. You guys were really quick—more than twice as fast as the San Francisco squad."

Erin and I glance at each other. We knew we were efficient, but we weren't exactly running between buildings. Oftentimes, we would stop in coffee shops to charge our phones or hang out in random buildings and parks. In other words, we could have gone even faster. What were the guys in San Francisco doing?

Lewis continues. "We've done a trial of the application with this information and it's a huge hit. The suburbs want it now as well. What do you think?"

Neither of us has anything else in the works, so we accept.

"Sounds like we're the elite team. Maybe you can just send us all over the world to stack markets."

Lewis says he would like to but it might not be feasible.

We thank him and head out, completing the downtown portion of the gig. As we walk to the train, I glance up at all of the buildings I have stacked over the past few weeks. I look at them like I did the mountains I hiked in Glacier National Park. At first, they look intimidating, but afterwards, just another obstacle conquered.

I get on the train to head home and know that the suburbs will be a cakewalk. Just as I have since the beginning of the job, I can't help but survey my surroundings. To my right, a man is reading *The New Yorker*. Several others are listening to music. One guy is drinking a Red Bull and nervously looking out the window. Maybe when I get home, I will start looking for jobs at the CIA—unless I am permanently on a blacklist from the incident a month earlier.

# EPILOGUE

When I tell people what I do for a living and regale them with stories about the jobs I have worked, many are envious. They work in cubicles, so participating in flash dances sounds incredible to them. But the problem with working these kinds of gigs is that you never know when the next one is coming, and ultimately the lifestyle is not sustainable. Most of the jobs detailed in this book were short-term positions, from the one-day flash dances to the five-month data collection job. And not a single one of these jobs offered any sort of benefits in the traditional sense—401K, paid time off, sick days, or health insurance. If you didn't work, you didn't get paid.

That's not to say the last three years have been completely miserable. After working six days a week at the mail sorting facility for several weeks, I was able to afford a trip to Miami to volunteer at the Sony Ericsson Open tennis tournament. My savings from the Glacier summer allowed me to take a trip to Peru in October of that year. Around holidays, I could take more days off than anyone working a typical job. My position collecting data for the obesity study allowed me free travel to unique places all over the country.

With that being said, my goal is to procure a full-time job, just as it has been since the summer of 2010. There is too much stress involved in struggling to pay rent on time, refusing to go to the doctor because of subpar, self-purchased health insurance, and constantly worrying about being out of work for extended periods of time.

Working these jobs, I realized that I was not alone in my situation. I met hundreds of people in the same boat. The vast majority of my coworkers were college graduates. Most of them were not working these jobs because they wanted to, but rather as a means to survive while trying to figure out something better.

The world is definitely changing faster than ever before and the next generation of workers in the United States will have to adapt. Every day in the news, there are more and more stories about the direction this country is headed. Collective bargaining agreements are being thrown out the window and salaries and retirement schemes are being slashed. Pensions are disappearing, and being replaced with 401Ks, which rely on the investment performance of a stock market seeing anemic growth. Health insurance costs are increasing at a rate much higher than that of people's wages. One-sixth of the population is on food stamps. Student scores on international tests continue to lag behind much of the developed world. Bridges and roads are collapsing and killing people because states don't have the money to fix them.

The list goes on and on. This country isn't as rich as it once was, and it will take something special to reverse course. Since a lot of jobs can be done for cheaper in other countries, the only way to improve the state of affairs will be to innovate and learn a skill people are willing to pay a living wage for.

For me, this means I will need to figure out if I should return to school to develop a niche skill in the modern economy, continue to look for an accounting or research job in Chicago, or perhaps move to a different country where there might be better work opportunities. Either way, I am not going to give up, even if things look bleak. If anything, these last three years have allowed me the chance to write about my experiences so that people can see how one person spent his time during the Great Recession.

# ACKNOWLEDGEMENTS

A lot of people supported me throughout this project. First off, I need to thank my parents for not pressuring me to get a "real" job and for being patient while I figure out what I need to do.

I have to thank my aunts, Pat and Jane, for being the first people to recommend that I keep writing and create a collection of stories after I sent them my initial mailroom piece.

I needed a lot of help editing. This process started with Josh Bald, Lindsay McNeill, and Laurie Koll. They spent countless hours reading through these stories, giving suggestions, and making several changes.

The second phase of editing was completed by Jessica Levesque, Frankie Huang, and Saria Bartholomew. Though it was frustrating seeing the manuscript get shredded, in the end, I believe the book needed it. This group spent a ton of time cleaning up everything and I sincerely appreciate their efforts. Frankie was also the talented illustrator that designed the cover that really captured the essence of the book.

I also need to thank Lyle Roebuck and Golden Krishna for their support and giving me feedback about the book and the publishing process.

I want to thank everyone that read my first several stories I sent out via email and for their comments and suggestions.

I need to thank Mike Brune, who edited and directed the Kickstarter video that helped finance this book. It immediately became a Staff Pick on the website because the video was so popular.

Finally, I must thank Fatima Musa, for being my best friend on the other side of the world, and being the only person that really gets me. She constantly asked me for project updates and made sure I finished the book. Your copy is on its way to Singapore.

A big thank you to all of my Kickstarter donors including:

Kenzie and Mike DeNardis, Jon "rb" Bauman, Anonymous (3), Douglas and Jennifer Chesna, Lyle Roebuck, Timur Selimkhanov, Nissly, Matt Berry, Elijah Edwards and Jennifer Cooper, Drew and Julie Rotschafer, Pamela and Paul Edwards, Cy Hendrickson, Erin Roberts, Dan Kresowik, Fatima Musa, David Geeslin, Destructo, Basil Mangra, Ian Kellar, Mark Edwards, Diana Dubuisson

## ABOUT THE AUTHOR

Andrew Edwards is from West Des Moines, Iowa, and currently resides in Chicago. In addition to working the jobs in this book, he has been a corn detasseler, golf club employee, paperboy, candy warehouse stocker, painter, focus group participant, snow shoveler, product tester, math tutor, grocery cashier, sandwich maker, courier, data entry clerk, soccer referee, warehouse worker, real estate accountant, store display designer, paper sorter, and science experiment participant. He plays ultimate competitively, loves listening to music, watches tennis religiously, and travels as often as he can. This is his first book.